D-DAY

D-DAY

Brigadier Peter Young

GALLERY BOOKS
An imprint of W.H. Smith Publishers Inc.
112 Madison Avenue
New York, New York 10016

Published by Gallery Books
A Division of W H Smith Publishers Inc.
112 Madison Avenue
New York, New York 10016

Produced by
Brompton Books Corp.
15 Sherwood Place
Greenwich, CT 06830

ISBN 0-8317-9647-2

Printed in Hong Kong

10 9 8 7 6 5 4 3 2 1

PAGES 2-3: *Preparing for D-Day.
Equipment belonging to elements of
the US 1st Infantry Division is
loaded on to assault barges at
anchor in the harbor of an English
south coast port.*

PAGE 5: *Heavily laden US
infantrymen begin their advance
inland from Omaha beach, 6 June
1944.*

CONTENTS

1 Countdown to Invasion   6
2 The Airborne Assault   26
3 The Opening Bombardment   36
4 Omaha and Utah   42
5 The British Landings   58
6 The Allies Victorious   70
   Appendix   78
   Index   79
   Acknowledgments   80

1
COUNTDOWN
TO INVASION

On 6 June 1944, in the greatest combined operation of all time, the Allies assaulted the strongly fortified coast of France, broke through the defenses and secured a lodgment. This, with the battle for Normandy that followed, must rank among the decisive battles of the world.

The assault was made at a time when the Germans were already fighting for their lives on the Eastern Front and when the Allies had already won mastery of both air and sea. Even so the result was far from being a foregone conclusion. The Allied troops who took part, though fairly well trained, were not for the most part very experienced. If the Allied leaders had proved their skill in former campaigns, the same must also be said of the German leaders, von Rundstedt and Rommel. However, the Allies had built up a remarkable partnership. Cooperation between the Americans and the British was close and efficient, and if this account emphasizes the part played by the two main Allies, it must be remembered that the Canadians, French, Poles, Belgians, Dutch, Czechs and the Yugoslavs all played a valiant part in the ultimate victory.

The Allies owed their success in large measure to the skills they had developed in the techniques of amphibious warfare. The British Combined Operations Headquarters had set new standards in interservice cooperation, masterminded by Lord Louis Mountbatten.

Allied industrial capacity ensured that their forces went into battle well armed and well equipped. Wars are won by fighting men; morale is even more important than weaponry. The campaigns in Sicily and Italy in 1943, allowed the Germans to demonstrate the skill and determination which had won them their great victories of the 1939-41 period. How would the young Allied warrior measure up to the German soldier of 1944? That was the question.

The Allies had made no secret of their intention to invade Europe, and as early as 1942 there had been a great deal of ill-informed pressure for a 'Second Front Now!' Sympathy for the Soviets and sheer ignorance of the Allies' unpreparedness contributed to this clamor. It has been argued that the invasion should have been launched in the summer of 1943, but few if any of those who held responsible positions on the Allied side were of that opinion at the time. When the blow eventually fell, the Germans had been preparing their defenses for the better part of four years.

The task of repelling the invasion fell to Field Marshal Karl Rudolf Gerd von Rundstedt, who in March 1942 was recalled from retirement for the second time and appointed Commander in Chief, West. His responsibilities included the defense of France, Belgium and Holland, the countries where the Allies were expected to launch their assault. He was answerable only to the Führer himself.

On 23 March 1942, in Directive No 40, Hitler laid down the defensive policy by which he intended to foil any Allied attack. Fortified areas were to be prepared in coastal sections exposed to a landing, and reserves were to be held ready for a counterattack. It was laid down that 'enemy forces which have landed must be destroyed or thrown back into the sea by immediate counterattack.'

Von Rundstedt had scarcely assumed command when, on 28 March, the British carried out a fierce raid on the naval base of St Nazaire. The great dock was put out of action, and Hitler, greatly displeased, ordered the construction of yet more formidable defenses. The results of the British and Canadian raid on Dieppe on 19 August confirmed the Führer's good opinion of the value of coastal fortifications. Von Rundstedt, for his part, believed in the more conventional strategy of a strong *masse de manoeuvre* held well back, but capable of launching a massive counterattack against an Allied beachhead.

Von Rundstedt was the supreme example of the orthodox general of the Prussian school. A little old fashioned perhaps, he was nonetheless the man given

PREVIOUS PAGES: *The buildup to the Allied invasion of Western Europe. Here, LCAs (Landing Craft, Assault) are put through their paces in preparation for the Normandy landings.*

LEFT: *Field Marshal Karl von Rundstedt, appointed Commander in Chief, West, by Hitler, was responsible for overseeing the defenses of northwest Europe before D-Day.*

the credit for having struck down France in the Blitzkrieg of 1940. From there he had gone on to the Soviet Union, but blunt criticism of the Führer's strategy had led to his replacement. He was greatly respected by the German officer corps, which helped him in his dealings with Hitler. He had a low opinion of his master – though

ABOVE: *British and Canadian prisoners are escorted away from the seafront at Dieppe, 19 August 1942. The raid was for the most part a disaster, but provided much valuable information on the difficulties of launching a seaborne assault against an occupied coast.*

RIGHT: *The scene on the Dieppe beaches after the raid. Loose shingle and a high sea wall prevented the supporting Churchill tanks from moving off the beaches. Enfilading fire caused heavy losses among the unsupported Canadian assault units.*

LEFT: *Some of the survivors of the Dieppe raid disembark at Newhaven. Commandos and a detachment of US Rangers (seen here) scored notable successes during the operation and, two years later, would be employed in a similar role on D-Day – the establishment of secure flanks on the invasion beaches.*

ABOVE RIGHT: *A Nazi propaganda photograph showing the massive reinforced concrete casement of a coastal battery, probably in the Pas de Calais area. In reality, Hitler's much-vaunted Atlantic Wall was far from complete by the summer of 1944.*

BELOW RIGHT: *The crew of an MG 34 machine gun scan the horizon for signs of a target.*

he had the wit to conceal it. His new job had its consolations; he enjoyed a civilized life at his headquarters in the Château de St Germain-en-Laye, overlooking the Seine. He needed something to make up for a task which he himself was to describe thus:

'I had over 3000 miles of coastline to cover from the Italian frontier in the south to the German frontier in the north, and only 60 divisions with which to defend it. Most of them were low-grade divisions and some of them were skeletons.'

Well versed in military history, von Rundstedt was familiar with Frederick the Great's dictum, 'Little minds want to defend everything; sensible men concentrate on the essential.' What were the essentials and, if he should succeed in selecting them, would Hitler let him develop his strategy unhindered? During 1943 it became evident that the answer to this last question was an emphatic no. Hitler was growing more nervous. General Gunther Blumentritt commented:

'He was constantly on the jump – at one moment he expected an invasion in Norway, at another in Holland, then near the Somme, or Normandy or Brittany, in Portugal, in Spain, in the Adriatic.'

At the tactical level the task of defending the Channel coast fell to Field Marshal Erwin Rommel, an officer of outstanding tactical skill. Rommel felt that 'the war will be won or lost on the beaches. The first 24 hours will be decisive.' Unfortunately for the Germans his ideas did not entirely coincide with those of von Rundstedt, upon whom the ultimate responsibility rested.

Rommel, unlike so many of the German generals, could boast no aristocratic origins. He was the son of a Bavarian schoolmaster. Commissioned in 1912 he had distinguished himself greatly in World War I, at platoon, company and battle group level. He had fought in turn against the French, the Rumanians and the Italians, always with outstanding success. Skill, courage, vigor and initiative were the hallmarks of his operations. His decorations included the highest, the Pour le Mérite. Rommel was fortunate in that his battle experience was not confined to the trench warfare of the Western Front. He did not belong to the school of thought which believed in limited advances following a barrage. His exploits in Rumania and Italy had shown him the value of speed and surprise to achieve deep penetration of an enemy position.

Rommel stayed on in the small army allowed to Germany by the Treaty of Versailles, rising to the rank of colonel, and commanding the Führer's bodyguard in the Sudetenland and in Poland in 1939. Convinced of the value of the tank in modern warfare, he asked for the command of an armored division, and was given 7th Panzer, which he led with notable élan in the Blitzkrieg of 1940. Thereafter his advancement was rapid for although Rommel was not a fanatical Nazi Hitler preferred him to the Prussian aristocrats, who had such a firm grip on the German General Staff.

In February 1941 Rommel, now a lieutenant general, was sent to Libya, where the Italians had been roughly handled in the so-called Wavell Offensive. During the next 18 months he built up a tremendous reputation as a tank commander in desert warfare. His capture of Tobruk on 21 June 1942 won him the field marshal's baton, and a reputation for invincibility. However, Auchinleck held him at El Alamein, and Rommel found himself far from his base, starved of supplies and suffering from a stomach ailment. On 23 October, when Rommel was in hospital in Germany, a new British general, Montgomery, fell upon his army and broke it in the long and bitter Battle of El Alamein.

Rommel's reputation survived the loss of North Africa and, after a spell in Italy, he was sent to inspect the defenses of northern France in November 1943. At first Rommel had no direct responsibility, and he felt that this made him ineffectual. He complained to Berlin and was given command of Army Group B under von Rundstedt. Although this clarified the chain of command it also revealed the fundamental difference in outlook of the two field marshals.

Von Rundstedt believed in a powerful, mobile armored reserve, a *masse de manoeuvre*, which would move against the invaders wherever they might choose to land. This was, of course, excellent theory. The lack of such a reserve had paralyzed Gamelin in 1940. Rommel, the great exponent of mobile warfare, had a far greater practical knowledge of handling tanks than von Rundstedt. Even so one might have supposed that his commander in chief's solution would have appealed to him. In fact Rommel had no faith in von Rundstedt's plan. It was not that he was abandoning the principles that had won him his desert successes. Practical tactician that he was, he simply appreciated that Allied air superiority would delay the armored reserve so much that it

would rob it of its mobility. It would not be able to move quickly enough to prevent the Allies securing a foothold, building up a bridgehead and eventually achieving a breakout. Under all the circumstances Rommel felt that the only hope was to prevent the Allies landing at all; to stop them on the beaches. This meant that a thin gray line, supported by armor spread out close to the coastline, must be organized so as to hurl back the Allies on D-Day, as had been done at Dieppe in 1942.

In fact the plans of the two field marshals were never really reconciled. Von Rundstedt continued to sit on his mobile reserves, while Rommel sped up and down the coast, inspecting units and fortresses, siting guns, inventing obstacles and gingering up the defenders with his considerable powers of leadership. With the benefit of hindsight one must concede that, given Allied domination of the skies above Normandy, Rommel's plan was more realistic than von Rundstedt's, however correct that may have been in theory.

During the period of rather more than two years between von Rundstedt's appointment and D-Day the forces at his command suffered considerable erosion. Every time the Germans suffered a setback elsewhere Hitler nibbled away at von Rundstedt's armies until their quality became decidedly uneven. That is not to say that von Rundstedt did not still have formations of superb military value. No soldier worth the name would underrate the 10 panzer divisions which formed the solid core of his forces.

One way of measuring the strength of Germany at the beginning of 1944 is simply to examine the layout of divisions in the field:

Eastern Front	179
France and the Low Countries	53
Balkan States	26
Italy	22
Scandinavia	16
Finland	8
	304

Of these, 24, stationed in the occupied countries, were still in the process of formation. Worse still, there was no general reserve in Germany. Hitler had a tremendous army at his command, but it was already committed. Only by robbing other fronts could he reinforce the West. Even so, the occupation forces were formid-

able. In wartime the ration strength of an army tends to be a good deal higher than its real strength. Not *all* quartermasters are honest. However that may be, on 1 March 1944 there were in France:

Army	806,927
SS and Police	85,230
Volunteers (foreign)	61,439
Allies	13,631
Air Force	337,140
Navy	96,084
Total	1,400,451
Armed Force Auxiliaries	145,611

Of the air force personnel over 100,000 were in Flak formations, and more than 30,000 were 'paratroops.' The Luftwaffe in the West under Field Marshal Hugo Sperrle had about 890 aircraft available for operations. Of these about 150 were reconnaissance and transport aircraft.

Vice-Admiral Kranke commanded Naval Group, West. Naval personnel manned a number of the key coastal batteries with radar equipment – thus complicating defense policy. The ships and craft available included a weak destroyer flotilla, some torpedo boats, a number of patrol craft and minelayers. There were U-boats based at Brest, and other Atlantic coast ports, but they were not under Kranke. These, in broad terms were the forces the Allies had to reckon with.

At the last meeting of the Cairo Conference, on 6 December 1943, President Roosevelt nominated General Dwight David Eisenhower as Supreme Allied Commander for Operation Overlord. Before he took up his new appointment, as he generously conceded later, Lieutenant General Frederick E Morgan had already 'made D-Day possible.'

At the Casablanca Conference in January 1943 the Allies had decided to set up a Combined Allied Staff to plan Overlord. The Chief of Staff to the Supreme Allied Commander (designate), Morgan, was British, and his deputy, Major General Ray W Baker, was a United States army officer. The organization became known as

ABOVE: *Field Marshal Erwin Rommel, commander of Army Group B, was placed in charge of the defenses along the Channel coast. Forced to work with limited resources, he was nevertheless able to improve the German fortifications along the coast. Here he inspects a concrete and steel device designed to rip open the hull of any assault craft. He is accompanied by Doctor Wilhelm Meise, his chief of engineers.*

LEFT: *An exterior view of a German artillery redoubt, somewhere along the Channel coast.*

RIGHT: *Crude but effective, a barbed-wire strewn antitank ditch. To combat such potentially lethal defenses, the British created the specialist beach-clearance 79th Armored Division, better known as the 'Funnies.'*

COSSAC. Morgan received his directive on 26 April 1943. This stated, 'our object is to defeat the German fighting forces in Northwest Europe.' It instructed COSSAC to prepare plans for a full-scale assault against the continent as early as possible in 1944, with 'an elaborate camouflage and deception scheme' extending over the summer of 1943 designed to pin the Germans in the West by keeping alive their expectation of an invasion that year. In the event of the Germans collapsing there was to be a plan ready so that whatever forces were available in the United Kingdom could immediately be sent to the continent. At the Trident Conference, held in Washington in May 1943, the target date for Overlord was set for 1 May 1944. COSSAC was given a list of the forces which, it was thought, would be available:

5 infantry divisions in assault vessels
2 follow-up infantry divisions
2 airborne divisions
20 divisions for movement into the lodgment area.

The capture and development of ports would permit the landing of divisions direct from America, or elsewhere, at a rate of from three to five a month.

RIGHT: *Allied leaders prepare for the invasion of Nazi-occupied Europe at the Casablanca Conference, January 1943. From left to right: Anthony Eden, Alan Brooke, Air Chief Marshal Tedder, Admiral Cunningham, General Alexander, General Marshall, General Eisenhower and General Montgomery. Prime Minister Churchill (center) pushed to establish a combined Allied staff at the meeting, a move that led to the creation of the body known as COSSAC.*

BELOW RIGHT: *The team that undertook the detailed preparations for Operation Overlord. From left to right, back row: Lieutenant General Omar Bradley, commander US First Army; Admiral Sir Bertram Ramsey, naval commander; Air Chief Marshal Sir Trafford Leigh-Mallory, commander of Allied air forces; and Lieutenant General Bedell Smith, chief of staff to Eisenhower. Front row: Air Chief Marshal Sir Arthur Tedder, deputy supreme commander; General Dwight D Eisenhower, supreme commander; and General Sir Bernard Law Montgomery, commander of land forces.*

The assault force of ships and landing craft would amount to some 3300 vessels. It seems a huge figure, but in fact shortage of landing craft was to plague the Allies until the end of the war in Europe. About 11,400 aircraft, including 632 transport planes for airborne operations, would be available.

In the first week of June General Morgan was told to submit his outline plan by 1 August 1943. That he was able to do so was due to Winston Churchill's aggressive policy which, even before Dunkirk, had called for raids on the enemy-held coast, and plans for an eventual return to France. The small organization under General A G B Bourne, Royal Marines, which in 1940 was charged with this task, had expanded under Admiral of the Fleet, Sir Roger Keyes. Later it expanded far more significantly under Vice-Admiral Mountbatten, whose Combined Operations Headquarters, though affiliated to the Admiralty, the War Office and the Air Ministry, was separate from them. Mountbatten, who held equivalent rank in all three services, sat as a member of the Chiefs of Staff Committee. He was the recognized authority on the planning and mounting of seaborne assaults, whether commando raids or full-scale invasions. The zeal and originality which Mountbatten brought to Combined Operations Headquarters permeated through to the staff of all three services in the planning of Overlord.

At the Quadrant meeting in Quebec in August 1943 the COSSAC plan, after being considered in turn by the British Chiefs of Staff and the American Joint Chiefs of Staff was finally submitted to Churchill and Roosevelt by their Combined Chiefs of Staff. It was accepted, with some useful modifications. Churchill urged that the force should be increased by at least 25 percent and that the assault front should be extended to include the eastern coast of the Cherbourg peninsula. The Combined

Chiefs, although they agreed that the force should be strengthened if possible, did not increase the allocation of ships and craft.

General Morgan was now given authority 'for taking the necessary executive action to implement those plans approved by the Combined Chiefs of Staff.' Since nearly four months were to pass before Eisenhower's appointment Morgan was working as Chief of Staff to an unknown Supreme Commander. All that was known was that, at Churchill's suggestion, he was to be an American, since the United States would eventually be providing a larger proportion of the Allied force.

Eisenhower was an admirable choice for Supreme Commander, not by virtue of battle experience in World War I – he had none – or outstanding strategic skill, but because his lack of personal ambition, his sincere, warm and friendly personality fitted him to run a team which included such idiosyncratic characters as Patton and Montgomery. Son of a Texan railroad worker, he was brought up in poverty, but won his way to West Point, and was commissioned in 1913. He served under the great General Douglas MacArthur in the Philippines, and later attracted the attention of General George C Marshall, who was Roosevelt's principal military adviser throughout the war. Eisenhower was hardly of the caliber of either of these giants, but he was an excellent chairman, and enjoyed great popularity with the British.

As Deputy Supreme Commander a British Air Chief Marshal, Sir Arthur Tedder, was chosen. He had already worked harmoniously with Eisenhower in 1943 when he had been Commander in Chief, Mediterranean Allied Air Forces. His success in planning and executing operations over Tunisia, Sicily and Italy made him an excellent choice, for it was evident that the air arm would be of paramount importance in the campaign ahead. Eisenhower considered him 'one of the few great military leaders of our time.' A Luftwaffe comment of the time is flattering:

'Tedder is on good terms with Eisenhower to whom he is superior in both intelligence and energy. The coming operations will be conducted by him to a very large extent . . . Obviously we are dealing here with one of the most eminent personalities among the invasion leaders.'

Not unnaturally, Eisenhower wished to retain his trusted Chief of Staff, Lieutenant General W Bedell Smith, who had been with him in North Africa, Sicily and Italy. Although he was Eisenhower's hatchet man, he could be disciplined as well as tough. Morgan, whose knowledge of how the COSSAC plan had developed was invaluable, became a deputy chief of staff.

The naval commander was Admiral Sir Bertram Ramsay, the man who brought the British Expeditionary Force (BEF) home from the beaches of Dunkirk. He had helped to plan the landings in North Africa in 1942, and had commanded the Eastern Naval Task Force in the assault on Sicily. He was a punctilious man who believed in attention to detail – there are enough hazards at sea without leaving things to chance when you do not have to. Nevertheless some of the American admirals were to be critical of the amounts of detail in his orders. Ramsay remained calm and urbane.

Command of the Allied Tactical Air Forces was given to Air Chief Marshal Sir Trafford Leigh-Mallory who, like Ramsay, had special qualifications for his role. After commanding 12 Group in the Battle of Britain, he had been the air force commander of the Royal Air Force School of Army Cooperation, and Air Officer Commanding in Chief, Fighter Command. He was prepared to stand up to 'the bomber barons.'

Command of the Allied forces, 21st Army Group, was given to General Sir Bernard Montgomery. Eisenhower wanted to have General Sir Harold Alexander, but the British government knew that the victor of El Alamein could not be lightly set aside. In any case Alexander had all the qualities required to run the very mixed team of Allies then slogging their way up Italy. So it fell to Montgomery to command the land forces in Overlord. He was a strange man, not really very likeable, though he had sufficient sense of humor to be amused by his own peculiarities, which, besides a brusque manner, included a direct line to the Almighty. Although he got on badly with some colleagues – Patton for one detested him – he had an almost magical influence on the British soldier. When Montgomery was in command the men thought they could not be beaten. Though a strong-minded, efficient, sound and relentless commander, it cannot be said that he was especially gifted as a strategist. However, in the spring of 1944 his chief reverse, at

Arnhem, still lay in the future. Thus far his road had been strewn with laurels. Had he not routed the great Rommel himself?

Command of the American First Army, which was one of the two assault armies, was in the safe hands of Lieutenant General Omar N Bradley. Commissioned in 1915, Bradley was made lieutenant colonel only in 1936, when he was already 43. During World War II promotion came rapidly, and in Tunisia and Sicily he had been a corps commander. He and Eisenhower had been friends since their West Point days, and the latter wrote of Bradley's 'ability and reputation as a sound, painstaking, and broadly educated soldier.' The newspapermen, led by Ernie Pyle, took a liking to him, and he became 'the GIs' General.'

The follow-up army of this group, the 12th Army Group, was the United States Third Army, under the dynamic and talented Lieutenant General George S Patton. His army took no part in the D-Day landing but its very existence was another worry for von Rundstedt.

The assault army of the 21st Army Group was the British Second Army, whose commander Lieutenant General Sir Miles Dempsey, had commanded a corps in Sicily and Italy. He was an exceptionally fine commander, but unlike most of his contemporaries he left no memoirs and is therefore comparatively little-known today. He was good-tempered, steady, confident and considerate, and was tremendously respected by all who knew him. He had a perfect understanding of the army he handled and had the knack of giving clear and precise verbal orders. Above all he had the ability to work with Montgomery, apparently without the least friction. Taken all round Dempsey was just about the ideal commander for the Second Army. Many a British general of far less worth has ended his career with a field marshal's baton in his hand!

The First Canadian Army, under Lieutenant General Henry D G Crerar was the follow-up army of

the 21st Army Group. It did not become operational until 23 July, but nevertheless its very existence had to be taken into account by the Germans.

RIGHT: *A group of French Resistance workers is briefed before an operation against a German target.*

BELOW: *A railroad junction and marshaling yard under attack from Allied bombers. To mislead the Germans as to the actual invasion front, the Allies ensured that two-thirds of their targets were outside the Normandy area.*

In a sense the Allies already had an army in Europe before D-Day, the Resistance. In theory the constitutional government was the Vichy regime under old Marshal Pétain. His authority had been greatly reduced and Pierre Laval, who secured the collaboration which the Germans demanded, governed only by their consent. By 1944 it was clear that the true voice of France was that of General Charles de Gaulle, whose headquarters was, of course, in London.

The French Resistance has been called 'a blend of courage and patriotism, ambition, faction and treachery.' It comprised numerous groups, whose political background varied from Communist and *Front Populaire* to Catholic. By 1944 the Maquis consisted of perhaps 100,000 people, many of whom had made their way to the mountains rather than be sent to Germany to work as conscript labor. They were the raw material for guerrilla war.

The Belgian Resistance, the 'Secret Army,' was some 45,000 strong. In the second quarter of 1944 55 air operations supplied it with arms. However, the *Abwehr* (German secret service) had been extremely successful in capturing Allied agents dropped into Holland, and the Dutch Resistance was still poorly equipped.

A complicated organization in England endeavored to control and to arm these Resistance movements. In this work the British Broadcasting Corporation and the Special Operations Executive (SOE) played an indispensable part.

The Allied planners, while agreeing that the flames of resistance must be fanned by every possible means, placed no reliance upon its activities. Any sabotage, or any armed rising, was simply to be regarded as a bonus. It is not easy to quantify the achievements of these patriotic men and women, but it is evident that they tied up thousands of enemy soldiers by their very existence. By ambush and sabotage they inflicted serious delays on the German reserves as they moved up to battle during the summer of 1944.

Besides armies that actually existed the Allies made good use of others that did not. It was essential to the

LEFT: *Generals Eisenhower and Montgomery attend the pre-invasion maneuvers of the US 3rd Armored Division, 25 February 1944.*

BELOW: *Four Mustang long-range escort fighters prepare to support a bomber raid on targets in northern Europe in the months before D-Day. Note the distinctive black-and-white 'invasion stripes.'*

success of Overlord that the Germans, who still enjoyed a great numerical advantage in land forces, should be led to make faulty dispositions. It was recognized, of course, that the German commanders were aware of Allied preparations for an assault. At the same time it was thought that, given good security, they might be deceived as to where and when the landing was to take place. For this reason it was essential that the preliminary bombing did not point to Normandy as the chosen beachhead. Therefore, for every target attacked in the actual assault area, two were bombed elsewhere,

especially in the Pas de Calais. This cover plan greatly increased the number of sorties which had to be flown by the Allied air forces, and therefore their casualties, but its strategic success cannot be doubted.

In order to misrepresent their overall strategy the Allies devised a deception plan (codenamed Bodyguard). This was supplemented by Fortitude which was the cover plan for Normandy. The story that the Allies tried to sell was that the campaign of 1944 would open with the invasion of southern Norway. Then, in about the third week of July, the main attack would be

RIGHT: *B-17 Flying Fortresses of the US Eighth Air Force head out on a daylight raid against French communication centers.*

BELOW: *US combat troops hit the beach during a training exercise, watched over by a US beachmaster, somewhere in southern Britain.*

launched against the Pas de Calais. Dummy landing craft were assembled in southeastern ports and harbors; radio traffic, training exercises and so on built up the desired impression. Even after D-Day the belief was encouraged that the attack on Normandy was a diversionary one.

The fictitious invasion of Norway was entrusted to Lieutenant General Sir A F A N Thorne, Commander in Chief, Northern Command. His 'Fourth Army,' consisting of three imaginary corps, was assembled in Scotland. There were *some* troops in Scotland, but for the

most part the Fourth was a phantom army, conjured out of the air by radio traffic from a skeleton headquarters consisting largely of signals staff. Troop movements and exercises, and some well-calculated leaks pointed to landings on the Norwegian coast. This deception was to be maintained until July. Hitler was sensitive to any threat to Norway. Infuriated by the commando raid which wiped out the garrison of Vaagso on 27 December 1941, he had built up the garrison of Norway to some 300,000 men. It was essential to the Allies that they should not be moved to France, where only 100,000 of

them would have added greatly to the defensive power of Army Group West. The Fourth Army was by no means the least effective of the armies that 'fought' on the Allied side in World War II.

The imaginary invasion of the Pas de Calais was scheduled for mid-July. A mythical assault force of 12 divisions was to be built up to 50 divisions. There were, of course, many real formations in east and southeast England. These made themselves appear even more formidable than they were by increasing the volume of radio traffic. Nothing was neglected that might add to the desired impression. Inspired leaks through the press, as well as through diplomatic and underground channels built up the picture. In the southeastern counties, forces – real and imaginary – were assembled openly, while in the southwest no effort of concealment was spared. German situation maps showing Allied dispositions in Britain prove the extent to which these deceptions worked.

Their success was helped by the fact that Hitler had been convinced at the outset that the Allies' main assault would come against the Pas de Calais. Indeed all the German leaders were convinced that it should be strongly guarded. This view was not unreasonable. It was the shortest sea route from England to France, and the shortest route for an Allied thrust at the industrial Ruhr. The German leaders thought it probable that the Allies would attack in several places, but opinions differed as to where the subsidiary assaults would land. Norway, the Atlantic coast, Portugal and the Mediterranean coast of France all came under discussion. In October 1943 von Rundstedt pointed out that 'Normandy with Cherbourg, and Brittany with Brest are additional important areas on the Channel front,' and, though it took him some time, it seems that Hitler came to think there was something in this. By 4 March he was describing them as 'particularly threatened' and two days later General Alfred Jodl, his personal Chief of Staff, told von Rundstedt that the Führer attached 'par-

ticular importance to Normandy,' and especially Cherbourg. This led to the reinforcement of the Cotentin peninsula by the 91st Airlanding Division, 6th Parachute Regiment and other units. In April the 21st Panzer Division was moved from Brittany to Caen and the Panzer *Lehr* Division from Hungary to Chartres, over 100 miles from the Normandy coast.

ABOVE: *US troops, possibly members of the 2nd Rangers, learn the techniques required to carry out a successful assault against a fortified cliff-top. The Rangers attacked German defenses on the Pointe de Hoe, to the west of Omaha, on D-Day.*

LEFT: *Files of British infantry advance inland after disembarking from their landing craft, May 1944. On D-Day the landings were much less ordered.*

RIGHT: *The lull before the storm. Members of a commando Special Service Brigade wait for the order to move out to their embarkation point on 3 June.*

Von Rundstedt's forecasts of Allied intentions were pretty sound. In his situation report of 15 May he emphasized the Allies' need to capture big harbors:

'Le Havre and Cherbourg are primarily to be considered for this purpose, Boulogne and the Cotentin peninsula in the first phase would therefore seem very natural. . . .'

On 29 May he concluded that the air attacks on the Seine bridges 'may indicate enemy designs on Normandy (formation of a bridgehead).'

The Allies, in fact, intended to land three airborne and five seaborne divisions between the River Dives and the Cherbourg peninsula, and to form a beachhead, which would include the towns of Caen, Bayeux and St

RIGHT: *A picture taken later in the day showing the commandos leaving their pre-invasion billets. The role of the commandos was to push inland from the invasion beaches and link up with the airborne forces which were dropped in advance of the main landings.*

Lô. The role of the airborne divisions was to secure the flanks of the beachhead, while the seaborne divisions pushed inland.

On the eve of the invasion there were three German infantry divisions guarding the beaches where the five Allied seaborne divisions were to land. Of these, the 709th and 716th Divisions were static and the 352nd Division was a field unit. In support south of Caen was the 21st Panzer Division, a powerful armored formation under Major General Edgar Feuchtinger.

The HQ of the German LXXXIV Corps was near St Lô. It was commanded by General Erich Marcks, a tall, scholarly looking man, who had lost a leg in Russia.

It may be doubted whether the German forces in the area selected for the Allied landing were in themselves sufficient to hurl the invaders into the sea. It cannot be said that either the 709th or 716th Divisions were particularly formidable formations. Much would depend on the handling of the 21st Panzer. Much more would depend on the speed with which these divisions could be reinforced. Some help might be expected fairly soon from the 711th Division, static though it was, and from the 77th Field Division. Although these might help to hold the ring, they were not likely to turn the tide of the battle. However, the Germans had three more armored divisions disposed where they might intervene in Normandy. These were the 116th Panzer, just east of the Seine, the 12th SS Panzer and Panzer *Lehr*. Much would depend on the speed with which the Germans could get all, or some, of these into the battle.

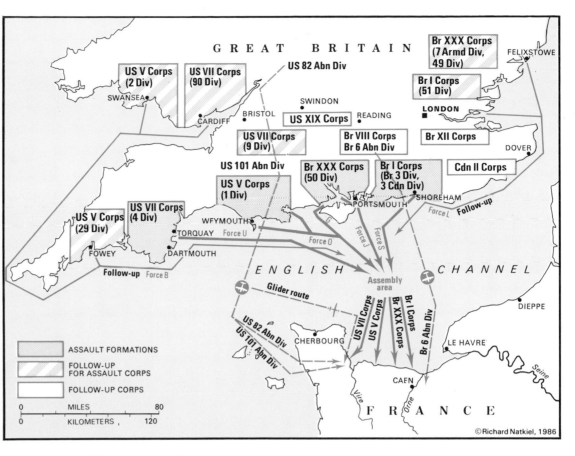

In May German air reconnaissance seldom reached even the south coast of England. Nevertheless, on 4 June Admiral Krancke expressed doubts as to 'whether the enemy has yet assembled his invasion fleet in the required strength.' Next day, Army Group B, with no fresh intelligence at hand but noting the concentration of Allied bombing between Dieppe and Dunkirk considered that it pointed to 'the previously assumed focal

point of the major landing' (the Pas de Calais). 'As yet,' wrote von Rundstedt that same day, 'there is no immediate prospect of the invasion.' Rommel left his headquarters to stay with his family for a night.

So, on the eve of D-Day the Germans were off their guard, the weather was foul in the Channel, and the eight Allied divisions were yearning to go. Why should 150,000 or so young men be so keen to stick their necks out? How did they come to be so well motivated? Every unit had been visited by the king or Ike, Monty, Dempsey, Bradley, or various other leaders, who had stressed the importance of the operation which was about to be launched. The British soldier is not lacking in cynicism, and this may well apply to the GI as well. The reason why the men were so eager to get cracking was that in the interests of security they had been assembled in tented camps, surrounded by barbed wire, where they had spent no less than a week. They had been allowed out only in formed groups, and had little to do but watch old films – *Claudia* springs to mind - and listen to a few more pep talks. The terrors of the West Wall were as nothing compared to a few more days in the Allied version of the concentration camp.

At 0415 hours on Sunday 4 June the Allied commanders in chief were told that the weather forecast for the 5th heralded poor visibility and low cloud over the beaches with rising seas in a mounting gale. Eisenhower had no alternative but to postpone the invasion for 24 hours. The bombarding warships on their way from Scotland had to turn back. The parts of Rear

RIGHT: *Landing craft, loaded with men and equipment of the 13th/18th Hussars, prepare to get underway.*

Admiral Kirk's convoy that were already on their way to the Utah assault area had to be recalled. Not until 0900 hours on Sunday 5 June was Admiral Ramsay certain that all units were on their way back to shelter.

At 2130 hours the commanders in chief met once more in the library at Southwick House. They were told that a break in the weather was coming. The rain in the assault area was going to clear up for 48 hours. The wind would drop, though the sea would still be rough and choppy. Heavy bombing would be possible on Monday night, 5 June. Another postponement would mean that D-Day would have to be put off for two weeks, with

all the ill effects that would bring to the assault troops who were keyed up for action.

Eisenhower asked each senior commander for his opinion. Leigh-Mallory and Tedder thought it would be 'chancey.' Ramsay – whose opinion in such a matter must have held great weight – thought that the assault should go ahead, and Montgomery agreed with him.

Eisenhower reflected for a while, and then made his decision:

'I am quite positive we must give the order. . . . I don't like it, but there is it. . . . I don't see how we can possibly do anything else.'

RIGHT: *The view from the bridge of a large transport. Note the escorting destroyer and pair of barrage balloons.*

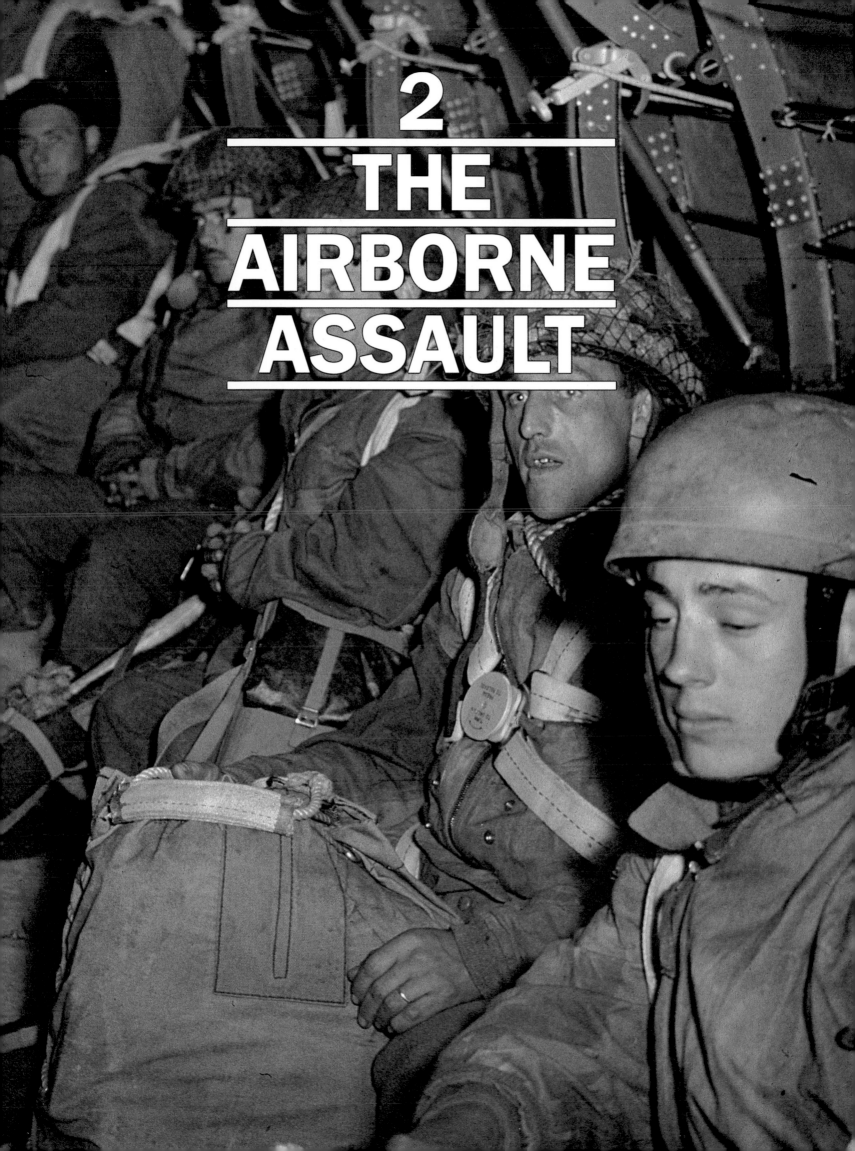

2
THE
AIRBORNE
ASSAULT

The airborne assault was a vital part of Operation Overlord. The Allies sent in three airborne divisions (see appendix for breakdown), two American and one British, to prepare for the main assault by taking certain strategic points and by disrupting German communications on the flanks of the beaches.

The task of the British 6th Airborne Division was to hold the eastern flank of the beachhead. This called for the seizure of the bridges over the River Orne, between Caen and the sea, and the capture of the Merville battery, which could enfilade the lodgment area, posing a dangerous threat to the left flank of the seaborne landings. In general it was intended to deny the Germans the rather rough tract of wooded and flooded country between the Rivers Orne and Dives. It was a tall order for a single division, even though it was to be reinforced by 1st Commando Brigade, which was to land from the sea.

Experience, especially in Sicily, had shown that landing parachutists and gliders on a windy night is a hazardous business. A large proportion of the troops engaged are certain to be dropped in the wrong place. Commanders who find themselves in the right place too often find themselves with no more than a handful of the troops allotted to their task. Lest this should seem too gloomy a picture it must be appreciated that the enemy commander, studying his map and marking every report of a hostile landing, will be doubly confused if some of the attackers have landed in the wrong place. The problem of where and when to launch the defenders' reserves – and there are never enough of these – becomes more intractable. So if some pilots lose their way, and if others release their gliders at the first burst of flak, some good may still come of it so long as the airborne troops do *something* on landing. The men of the 6th Airborne Division, as the Germans soon learned, would make a nuisance of themselves wherever they landed!

Major R J Howard was charged with the surprise capture of the Bénouville and Ranville bridges. His party comprised five platoons of the 2nd Oxfordshire and Buckinghamshire Light Infantry and 30 officers and men of the 249th Field Company, Royal Engineers. They crossed the French coast just after midnight, and six Horsa gliders were released. The first stuck its nose into the German wire surrounding the Bénouville bridge, and two others touched down within 100 yards. Two of the other gliders landed within 150 yards of the Ranville bridge. Both bridges were rushed and within 15 minutes had been taken, intact. Casualties were light, though the leading platoon commander was killed. The sappers found that the bridges had not been prepared for demolition. German prisoners from the 736th Grenadier Regiment of the 716th Infantry Division were taken.

To have taken the bridges was a great exploit, but unless they could be held there would be no communication with the troops, who landed east of the Orne. Howard took up a defensive position about the bridges. There was a good deal of desultory firing for there were German troops in the nearby villages of Bénouville and Ranville. A troop of three tanks approached, but was discouraged when the leader was hit by a PIAT (Projector Infantry Anti-Tank). The PIAT weighed 34.5 pounds and was a short-range weapon. It hurled a 2.5-pound bomb and was supposed to be effective at 100 yards, but it is thought that its successes were, generally speaking, scored at point-blank range.

A little later the German officer in command of the bridge defenses drove up in his car and was captured. This classic *coup de main* had been pulled off without one of the six gliders, which, released too far east, had landed eight miles from the target.

The task of the 3rd Parachute Brigade was to cut the bridges over the River Dives, so as to delay German

PAGES 26 AND 27: *Paratroopers of the British 6th Airborne Division await the signal to jump. Their mission on D-Day was to secure a number of important river crossings to the east and south of Sword beach and neutralize several German strongpoints.*

BELOW LEFT: *Prime Minister Churchill and General Eisenhower inspect the US 101st Airborne Division, the 'Screaming Eagles,' in late March 1944.*

RIGHT: *General Eisenhower chats informally with a paratrooper. Along with the US 82nd Airborne Division, the 'Screaming Eagles' were to be dropped inland from Utah beach on the eve of D-Day.*

BELOW: *British gliders lie scattered across a field north of the village of Ranville. The tail sections were designed to be removed rapidly to facilitate the deployment of men and their equipment.*

troops advancing to attack the British left flank. It was to occupy the high ground commanding these approaches, and to capture the Merville battery. The task of the 5th Parachute Brigade was to capture and hold the Orne crossings.

Every operation of war, however successful, has its share of *friction de guerre* (grit in the works). A typical example of this complicated operations for the 3rd Brigade. A pathfinder party which was to land on Drop Zone K was dropped in error on Zone N where, in all innocence, it began to send out the code letter K and to call in more troops of the 3rd Brigade. It was some time before this mistake could be put right.

The 5th Brigade was carried in 129 aircraft. All but five dropped their troops, but they were greatly dispersed and much time was lost while searching for equipment containers in the dark, and while trying to find the rendezvous.

LEFT: *US paratroopers pictured before a training jump.*

ABOVE: *An aerial view of a glider landing zone, somewhere to the northeast of Caen.*

It was 0130 hours before half the 7th Battalion and 591st Parachute Squadron, Royal Engineers, found their way to the rendezvous, without many of their machine guns, mortars and radios. They were sent to reinforce Major Howard. There was confused fighting in the villages of Bénouville and le Port, and the Germans actually overran the Regimental Aid Post, killing the chaplain! When dawn came the fighting was still going on, but the vital bridges were still in British hands.

The task of 12th Battalion was to hold the eastern approaches to the Ranville bridge. Fifteen of its 32 aircraft dropped their passengers accurately. Seven others were less than a mile out. The other 10 were wildly adrift. By 0400 hours the battalion had occupied Le Bas de Ranville and taken prisoners from 736th Grenadier Regiment.

Meanwhile 13th Battalion, whose task was to take Ranville and, with some sapper units, to clear and improve Drop Zone N, had taken its objective. They had also captured some men of 125th Panzer Grenadier Regiment, which belonged to 21st Panzer Division, stationed southeast of Caen.

At about 0330 hours the 68 Horsas of the third flight crossed the coast. Fifty – 25 of them somewhat damaged by flak – landed with few casualties. Low cloud now obscured the coast and some of the 18 missing gliders were simply lost. In other cases, no doubt, the towropes had parted. This wave brought in nine 6-pounder and two 17-pounder antitank guns, heavy engineer stores and equipment, and Major General Richard Nelson Gale. One may imagine his relief when he learned that

the *coup de main* had been successful, and that the bridgehead was holding out.

Meanwhile 3rd Brigade, though widely dispersed, had been carrying out a variety of tasks. The commander of 8th Battalion, with 160 men who had landed correctly on Zone K, had taken up a position on the high ground southwest of the Bois de Bavent, so as to cover a party which was demolishing the Bures bridge. Troops that had landed by mistake in Zone N also made for the high ground west of the Bois de Bavent. Most of 3rd Parachute Squadron was sent to blow the Bures bridge, but Major J C A Roseveare, with an officer and seven sappers, crowded into a jeep and trailer full of explosives and made for Troarn. At the entrance to the village they ran into a barbed-wire knife-rest. In the dark it took them 20 minutes to clear this obstacle out of the way. They sent out a scout, who shot a German cyclist. The garrison stood to arms. The jeep dashed through the village with 'a Boche in every doorway shooting like mad.' Firing back, they hurtled down the slope to the river and, astonishingly, they only lost one man on their reckless ride. Working as fast as they could they blew a wide gap in the center span of the bridge. Abandoning the jeep they made their way across country and rejoined their party, which had blown the Bures bridge, swimming several small streams on the way.

The Canadian battalion had a stiff fight at Varaville and captured the château there, though a pillbox held out. A valiant Frenchman, putting on a red beret, armed himself with a rifle and is credited with slaying three snipers in the nearby woods. Here, as at Amfreville and the other villages of this area, the civilians came out to tend to the wounded.

By far the worst task that fell to 3rd Brigade was the destruction of the Merville battery. It was thought that it had four guns. If it was not destroyed before daylight it would command the beaches on which 3rd Infantry Division and 1st Commando Brigade were to land. L F Ellis in Volume I of *Victory in the West* describes the position:

'The guns were in steel-doored concrete emplacements six feet thick, two of which were also covered by twelve feet of earth. They were in a fenced area of seven hundred by five hundred yards within which was a belt of barbed wire, double in places, fifteen feet thick and five feet high. An anti-tank ditch was incomplete but mines had been sown profusely and there were a dual-purpose gun position and about fifteen weapon pits. Outside the main position was a wired in strongpoint with five machine-gun emplacements and several other antiaircraft gun positions.'

(It so happens that the author was in this position two days later. Believe me it was a stinker.) The task of destroying the position fell to Lieutenant Colonel Terence Otway and the 9th Parachute Battalion. It would have been difficult enough had the whole operation gone according to plan. The intention was to use a small reconnaissance party and three companies. One, which was to be a firm base on which to rally, was to make a diversion against the main entrance. A second was to breach the defenses. A third was to make the assault. As a sort of bonus, a party, carried in three gliders, was to crash land on the battery just as the assault went in. All this was to be accomplished in four and a half hours of darkness. It was not an easy task.

The reconnaissance party dropped as planned and set off for the battery. That was just about all that *did* go according to plan. Much equipment was lost in the flooded area round Varaville, and only half the battalion dropped within a mile of the rendezvous. At 0255

hours Otway set off with 150 men. He arrived to find that his reconnaissance party had done rather well. They had cut the outer wire, marked paths through the minefield *with their feet*, and dealt with a number of booby traps.

ABOVE RIGHT: *A paratrooper poses for the camera before entering his transport aircraft. His equipment includes a 2.36-inch M1 rocket-launcher, better-known as the 'Bazooka.'*

RIGHT: *The shattered cockpit of an Allied glider, the result of a difficult landing or German resistance.*

200 yards away. Their troops engaged the Germans in the perimeter defenses.

Otway's seven parties went into action; the wire was breached and the main gate stormed. The garrison was overwhelmed in a brief and bloody assault. The 75mm guns were put out of action. Then the battalion's signal officer took 'a somewhat ruffled pigeon' from his pocket and sent it off to England to report the success. The bird was probably glad to leave.

This assault cost Otway's party 70 casualties. With the 80 survivors he made for his next objective, the high ground at Le Plein. In German hands this would have given their gunners wonderful observation posts, overlooking 3rd Infantry Division's area.

So, when dawn came 6th Airborne Division could claim that, despite every sort of accident, it had carried out all its main tasks. The Orne bridges were held. Three of the bridges over the Dives – Troarn, Bures, and Robehomme – had been blown, as well as another over a tributary at Varaville. The Merville battery was out of action. The beginnings of a defensive position was being formed on the high ground that runs from Le Plein to Troarn; vital ground. If the Germans could reconquer the area between Dives and the Orne they could render the beachhead untenable, and drive the Allies back into the sea.

At 0840 hours the 1st Commando Brigade under Brigadier Lord Lovat, DSO, MC, began to land west of Ouistreham. By midday the leading commando, 6, had reached the Bénouville bridge. It was deployed to strengthen the line on the high ground at Le Plein. This brigade, some 2000 strong, consisted of 3, 4, 6 and 45 (Royal Marine) Commandos.

Meanwhile two American airborne divisions, 82nd and 101st, had been dropped all over the Cotentin peninsula. Their task was to aid the assault of the United

Otway organized his men into seven parties. Two were to breach the main wire, four were to deal with the four guns and one was to make a diversion at the main entrance. At this juncture two of the Albemarles appeared, and flew around looking for the place to crash land. It had not been possible to put out lights to guide them, but eventually the gliders were released, landing

ABOVE LEFT: The scene at one of the US landing sites in the Cotentin peninsula on the morning of D-Day. Dakota tugs prepare to cut free from their gliders.

LEFT: 'Screaming Eagles' photographed on their way to Normandy. The pre-battle tension is clearly etched in their faces. Their equipment includes Garand M1 rifles, an M1 Thompson submachine gun and an M3 'Grease Gun.'

States First Army and facilitate the capture of the vital Cotentin peninsula. It was an ambitious plan. Some 18,000 men were to be dropped by night into an area of Normandy bocage and floods. The German defenders were more numerous than in the tract of country between the Orne and the Dives. The German troops were

mostly from 91st Division. This unit had been specially trained to combat airborne attacks.

In order to avoid the antiaircraft defenses of Cherbourg the American IX Troop Carrier Command made an indirect approach via the Channel Islands. They were protected by Mosquitos of Air Defence of Great Britain, while Stirlings of Bomber Command dropped 'window' (sheets of foil) so as to deceive the German radar. The bombers went on farther south to simulate diversionary landings.

As soon as the airborne forces turned east and crossed the coast of the Cotentin peninsula they ran into heavy flak and small-arms fire. There was thick cloud and formations tended to break up; even the pathfinders found it difficult to identify their targets. In consequence the drops were widely scattered. In *Cross-Channel Attack* G A Harrison describes the scene:

'The first actions of all airborne units in the Cotentin on D-Day were attempts by small groups of men to carry out in the fog of the battlefield their own portion of the assigned plan. There could be little overall direction from above.'

The accounts of what they achieved, especially those of 101st Airborne, are thin indeed. *Time* magazine supplements the official records. An officer told of seeing German tracer ripping through men's parachutes as they descended. In *D-Day* Warren Tute relates that:

'In one plane, a soldier laden with his 90 pounds of equipment got momentarily stuck in the door. A 20mm shell hit him in the belly. Fuse-caps in his pockets began to go off. Part of the wounded man's load was TNT. Before this human bomb could explode, his mates behind him pushed him out. The last they saw of him, his parachute had opened and he was drifting to earth in a shroud of bursting flame.'

General Matthew B Ridgway, the commander of 82nd Airborne Division, parachuted to earth and, collecting

ABOVE: *The bullet-damaged remains of an Allied glider, the victim of German flak, lies by the side of a Normandy road.*

RIGHT: *US paratroopers move through the main street of a Normandy village (St Marie-du-Mont) after linking up with the US 4th Infantry Division on Utah beach.*

LEFT: *Weary paratroopers take a break from mopping-up operations in the village of St Marcouf to the north of Utah beach.*

BELOW LEFT: *A German prisoner, wounded in the shoulder by smallarms fire, receives first aid and a cigarette from a corporal of the 82nd Airborne Division, Ste. Mère Eglise.*

11 officers and men, set up his HQ in an orchard. He wrote:

'The Germans were all around us, of course, sometimes within 500 yards of my command post, but in the fierce and confused fighting that was going on all about they did not launch the strong attack that could have wiped out our eggshell perimeter defenses.'

The 82nd Airborne was meant to be dropped astride the Merderet, to capture Ste Mère Eglise and to facilitate the advance into the Cotentin. Only one regiment was

dropped at all accurately and in a brilliant action a party from this unit quickly seized and held the village. The other troops of the division were scattered up to 25 miles away; many were left struggling in the marshy ground on either side of the Merderet.

The 101st Division was also widely dispersed but senior officers were able to collect parties and move toward the causeways inland from Utah which were their main objectives. Other groups managed to take bridgeheads over the Douve which would later be important in allowing a link with the Omaha forces. Although at dawn perhaps only 1000 of the division's men were under command they did manage to give valuable aid to the forces moving inland from Utah.

Chaos reigned in the Cotentin that night. Everywhere the paratroopers – their efforts supplemented by French saboteurs – were cutting the telephone lines. Even so news of the first landings got through to LXXXIV Corps HQ at St Lô:

'At 0111 hours – unforgettable moment – the field telephone rang. Something important was coming through; while listening to it, the General [Marcks] stood up stiffly, his hand gripping the edge of the table. With a nod, he beckoned his Chief of Staff to listen in. "Enemy parachute troops dropped east of the Orne estuary. Main area Breville-Ranville and the north edge of the Bavent Forest. Countermeasures are in progress." '

This message, which came from 716th Division (Lieutenant General W Richter) galvanized Marcks' HQ. 'The Corps Command post resembled a disturbed beehive,' wrote one of its staff officers, 'Priority messages were sent in all directions.' Marcks, in no doubt that this was the invasion, sent out the signal 'Alarm coast,' and between 0111 hours and dawn the warning went by field telephones to his units and formations. The information

RIGHT: *Paratroopers prepare to move out of St Marcouf to begin clearing the Cotentin peninsula of its German defenders.*

was passed to OKW (Armed Forces High Command) and to von Rundstedt's GHQ.

At OKW Field Marshal Wilhelm Keitel thought that the landing in Normandy must be a diversion. The real invasion would come at Calais. He was not going to wake the Führer for a false alarm. A better general than he, von Rundstedt, also believed this was a diversion and that the real blow was still to come – in the Pas de Calais.

In the prevailing confusion it was not strange that some of the generals on both sides simply did not know what was going on. Falley of the 91st Airborne Division went to find out for himself and was ambushed by American paratroops. This was reported to Ridgway whose comment was:

'Well, in our present situation, killing Divisional Commanders does not strike me as being particularly hilarious.'

RIGHT: *An apprehensive German surrenders to a US paratrooper. Although some of the defenders capitulated, others fought on with great determination.*

3
THE OPENING
BOMBARDMENT

As the assault fleet butted its way through the gale in the Channel, and the airborne divisions flew into France, the heavy aircraft of Bomber Command set off to attack the 10 most dangerous coast-defense batteries. Three of them had to be attacked early on, for Allied airborne troops would be landing near them soon after midnight. These were the Merville battery and those at Fontenay and St Martin de Varreville in the Cotentin. The other seven were to be bombed between 0315-0500 hours, so that they would scarcely have time to recover before dawn, when the naval bombardment would begin. These were the batteries at La Pernelle, Maisy, Pointe du Hoe, Longues, Mont Fleury, Ouistreham and Houlgate.

On average each battery received 500 tons of bombs delivered by about 100 aircraft. Of 1056 Lancaster, Halifax and Mosquito aircraft 11 did not return and 70 crew were lost.

Meanwhile in the ships and landing craft the invaders were spending a truly horrible night, thrown about by the violence of the gale, and for the most part seasick. As their craft pitched and rolled veterans of Sicily took what comfort they could from the thought that rough weather tended to put the Germans off their guard. Indeed, both at sea and in the air the Germans remained totally inactive. No aircraft seems to have spotted the assault fleet streaming into the Channel as darkness fell. No watcher on the coast of Normandy seems to have observed the Allied minesweepers at work.

Meanwhile two bomber squadrons, fitted with radar-jamming equipment, were masking the Germans' warning system. To add to the confusion dummy airborne landings were being made at Mattot, Marigny and Yvetot, the last being intended to suggest that an attack north of the Seine was planned. Feints by motor

launches and aircraft were made near Boulogne and in the Dieppe and Le Havre area, but there seems to have been little enemy reaction.

Soon after 0500 hours the British bombarding squadrons, guided in by the midget submarines *X20* and *X23* which were flashing green lights to seaward, began to take up their positions, and at about 0530 hours the fleet opened fire. Fifty miles of the Normandy coast rocked as salvo after salvo of heavy shells tore into the fortifications of the West Wall, and as ton after ton of bombs hailed down from the sky. One can imagine the Germans, many of them alerted soon after midnight by messages from LXXXIV Corps, peering through the

PREVIOUS PAGES: *Two ships of the Allied fleet that assembled for D-Day. The USS* Nevada *(foreground) shelled a German battery at Azeville; the* Texas, *supported the US Rangers during their assault on Pointe du Hoe.*

ABOVE: *The invasion fleet pictured during its untroubled crossing of the Channel on 6 June.*

LEFT: *P-38 Lightnings head for the Channel to cover Allied shipping. Four squadrons were committed on D-Day, when they flew combat air patrols over the mine-free paths along which the assault craft sailed.*

loopholes of their fortifications and trying, despite smoke and debris, to make out the ships and craft bearing down upon the beaches.

The bombardment fell upon the German defenders and the French inhabitants alike. The French, for the most part, stayed in their homes, even when these overlooked the beaches. At Ver sur Mer an elderly couple was found dead in bed, without a scratch on either of them. On 6 June 1944 an enormous weight of bombs and shells was delivered in the space of a few hours. It was a crucial phase of the operation and, of course, a tremendous encouragement to the men in the landing craft as they ran in, head-on, to sample whatever the West Wall might have in store for them.

With the dawn, wave after wave of day fighters began to come over, spreading out across the whole battlefield, ready to engage enemy aircraft or army reinforcements. A ceaseless patrol by four squadrons of Lightnings was kept up over the mine-free lanes which had been swept across the Channel. Thirty-six squadrons of Spitfires ensured that there were always six squadrons giving low cover over the assault area. Above the clouds, at about 8000 feet, three out of 16 squadrons of American Thunderbolts maintained a constant patrol. There were 30 reserve squadrons, which had six ready at all times as an immediate striking force. This mass of aircraft flew overhead unchallenged. Not a single German plane intervened during the first six hours of the invasion. There were Dunkirk veterans in the invasion force – not very many perhaps, but some. To them the air situation was a pleasant change.

Under this unparalleled air cover the warships came in to bombard. On the exposed eastern flank HMSs *Warspite, Ramillies* and *Roberts* opened fire, at about 0530 hours, with their 15-inch guns upon the batteries east of the Orne, at Villerville, Bénerville and Houl-

gate. It was an unforgettable sight. Battleships, cruisers, destroyers and support landing craft were engaging targets all along the British front. Admiral Krancke complained in his war diary that 'it was only to be expected that no effective blow could be struck at such a superior enemy force,' but in fact the German Navy did-

ABOVE RIGHT: *Decked out in black-and-white invasion stripes, a Martin Marauder medium bomber heads for Utah to pave the way for the assault troops.*

RIGHT: *LCIs (Landing Craft, Infantry) of the US Coast Guard head for Normandy protected by barrage balloons. Thanks to surprise and total control of the Channel skies, the Allies were not unduly troubled during the journey.*

LEFT: *The scene aboard a fighter-direction ship during D-Day. The map shows areas of major Allied air activity in support of the landings.*

BELOW: *A US battleship unleashes a broadside against a German target shortly before the first assault troops hit the beaches.*

strike back. Allied aircraft had laid a smoke screen to shield the anchorage from the heavy batteries at Le Havre. Three enterprising German torpedo boats dashed through the screen and sank the Norwegian warship *Svenner* before disappearing into the smoke. This startling attack was the only maritime riposte the enemy made that morning.

For the most part the fire of the German coast defense batteries was desultory and ineffective. However, the four-gun battery at Longues, though engaged by *Ajax* at 0530 hours, opened up on the headquarters ship, *Bulolo*, at about 0600 hours. It was silenced by 0620 but it reopened fire later and compelled *Bulolo* to move seaward. The cruisers *Ajax* and *Argonaut* then took on the battery. It received 179 shells, and two of its guns were

put out of action by direct hits through the embrasures. By 0845 hours the battery was silenced. The Bénerville battery, though silenced at the outset by *Ramillies*, opened up later and compelled *Warspite* to move her berth. To their credit it must be said that there were some determined German fighters at Longues and Bénerville.

By this time a fantastic regatta had begun. All along the front the assault craft were manned and lowered into the choppy sea for the final run in. In the American sector 269 medium bombers, Marauders of the Ninth Air Force, flew over to blast the defenses of Utah and silenced most of them. Bad visibility over the other beaches precluded pinpoint visual attacks on batteries and strongpoints. Instead wave after wave of aircraft

RIGHT: *The forward 14-inch guns of the USS* Nevada *in action on D-Day.*

BELOW: *A B-26 Martin Marauder of the US Ninth Air Force returns to England after dropping its bombs on German positions. Below lies Utah beach.*

flew in, in line abreast, releasing their bombs on the orders of pathfinders aiming by instruments.

About five minutes before H-Hour some 38,000 five-inch explosive rockets deluged the beaches. They were fired electrically from assault craft, each of which was capable of launching 1000 rockets in 90 seconds. As their salvoes finished exploding the first seaborne soldiers of the invading armies set foot on shore.

4
OMAHA
AND
UTAH

The American landings were made on Utah and Omaha. Utah proved to be the easiest landing, and Omaha the most difficult of the whole Allied assault. The Utah beaches, on the east coast of the Cotentin, were assailed by VII Corps under Lieutenant General J L Collins. The Omaha beaches, between Vire and Port en Bessin were attacked by V Corps under Lieutenant General L T Gerow.

The Americans had decided to go in at 0630 hours, about an hour earlier than the British owing to the difference in tides. At low tide it would be easier to clear the obstacles. The naval bombardment was not to open until 0550, 20 minutes later than on the British front. The defenses on the beaches where the British landed suffered two hours bombardment before H-Hour, as opposed to only 40 minutes on the American front. With the benefit of hindsight Admiral Kirk, commanding the Western Task Force, commented that:

'the period of bombardment was extremely heavy but was of too short duration to silence or neutralize all the defenses, particularly in the Omaha area.'

Rear Admiral Hall was of the same opinion:

'the time available for the prelanding bombardment was not sufficient for the destruction of beach defense targets.'

Another major difference between the American and British plans was the choice of the lowering positions ('transport areas'), where the troops transferred from ships into landing craft. The American lowering position was 11 miles from the coast, the British only seven. The American soldiers running in to Utah or Omaha had to put up with three hours in small craft in rougher conditions than any they had met with during training. For those approaching Utah this was not so bad for their run in was sheltered under the lee of the Cotentin peninsula. Force U had one piece of bad luck. It ran into an undetected minefield, and lost the navigational leader of the lefthand assault group, which had four DD (amphibious) tanks aboard, and the destroyer, *Corry*.

The US 4th Infantry Division made the opening attacks on Utah. By mistake the landings all took place on the southern part of the beach which happened to be less well defended. The landing began punctually at 0630 hours against slight opposition, which was quickly overcome. The 28 DD tanks still available swam in 3000 yards and landed safely some minutes behind the infantry. The engineers and naval demolition parties set to work to destroy the beach obstacles, and cleared them within an hour, giving landing craft a clear run in. This was an achievement which could not be paralleled anywhere else on the whole front.

The infantry now pushed inland with the object of capturing the causeway roads leading to Pouppeville, Ste Marie du Mont and Audouville la Hubert. Meanwhile, follow-up troops, vehicles and equipment were coming in unopposed, their movement inland was delayed only by the lack of beach exits and the need to breach the sea wall separating the land from the shore.

The first contact between American seaborne and airborne troops took place near Pouppeville, which was attacked at about 0800 hours by a small party of parachutists. Some of the garrison held out until noon.

By 1000 hours there were six battalions ashore and progress inland was delayed by flooding rather than German opposition. This is not to say that there was no resistance. Still, by a combination of accidents some of the leading assault craft missed the stronger German defenses. The mining of the vessel guiding them in and the strong current sweeping down the shoreline

PAGES 42-43: *US landing craft begin their run-in to the beaches. The attack began at 0630 hours, after the 40-minute naval bombardment. The craft had to cross up to 11 miles of choppy seas before they could drop their cargoes of men and equipment.*

RIGHT: *Members of the US 1st Infantry Division huddle behind the protective bow ramp of their assault craft as they near Omaha. The beach is already littered with swamped and disabled vehicles, suggesting that these men are part of the second wave*

brought them in several miles south of their planned landing place. Brigadier General Theodore Roosevelt Jr, a veteran aged 57 who had persuaded his divisional commander to let him go ashore 'to steady the boys,' took the vital decision to push inland, deepening the beachhead for the follow-up troops. Ably supported by Commodore James Arnold, the naval officer in charge of the beachhead, he solved the traffic problem, bringing in troops on Green beach, instead of getting them massacred on Red. It took the Germans three hours to shift their fire and by that time men of the 4th Division were pushing toward Ste Mère Eglise, where the strongest concentration of the 82nd Airborne Division was centered. Force U had landed about 23,250 men

LEFT: *The USS* Arkansas *fires on suspected German positions in the vicinity of St Laurent, a village slightly inland from the central sector of Omaha beach.*

RIGHT: *Damaged by German shellfire, a landing craft begins to sink by the stern. In the distance are the larger transports which ferried the infantry to their marshaling areas.*

LEFT: *US troops wade ashore through light surf at Utah. By luck the landings occurred on the southern sector of the beach which was less well defended, allowing the 4th Infantry Division assault waves to move inland quickly.*

with 1742 vehicles and 1695 tons of stores. Although there was room for the buildup at Utah to proceed, the American VII Corps had not yet crossed the River Merderet to the west or pushed southward to join hands with the V Corps at Omaha. There was still a strong German group between Turqueville and Fauville, and a battle group from their 91st Infantry Division, trying to push down the Cherboug-Carentan road to Ste Mère Eglise, was meeting with stubborn resistance from a small detachment of 82nd Airborne Division at Neuville au Plain.

The 101st Airborne Division was having a difficult time. Of 32 gliders bringing reinforcements, 11 landed in or near Hiesville as planned, but many crashed or fell into the hands of the Germans. Although detachments covered the bridges at La Barquette and near Brévands,

LEFT: *Follow-on forces disembark at Utah. Equipment on the shoreline includes a DUKW amphibian and two halftracks towing 57mm antitank guns.*

RIGHT: 'Double Trouble,' a Sherman bulldozer modified for amphibious operations, moves forward to clear a way off one of the US invasion beaches.

between the sea and Carentan, two battalions of the German 6th Parachute Division, counterattacking from that town, had infiltrated between them and the rest of the 101st Division.

The landing craft plowing toward Omaha were buffeted by a stronger wind and rougher seas than Force U had encountered off Utah. The land behind the sand dunes at Utah is only a few feet above sea level, but Omaha beaches are overlooked by bluffs which rise in places to 150 feet and command the beaches. Whereas, the Utah defenses had been well and truly battered from air and sea, those at Omaha had been missed by the bombers. They were protected from seaward and the 40-minute naval bombardment had been unable to silence the guns. To make matters worse the German troops at Omaha, the 352nd Infantry Division, were not

RIGHT: US troops take shelter behind an earth embankment. The machine gun is a .3-inch Browning.

LEFT: *Members of the 4th Infantry Division push toward the village of St Marcouf to link up with Allied airborne forces in the area. By 1000 hours on D-Day six battalions had been landed on Utah; their progress was delayed by flooding rather than heavy German opposition.*

BELOW: *US transport aircraft fly in reinforcements to support the 101st and 82nd Airborne Divisions. Although both divisions had been scattered over a wide area during their descent, small units harried the German defenders with great success.*

only more numerous than those of the static 709th Division defending Utah, they were also better soldiers. Moreover, their defensive position, naturally strong, had been skillfully fortified. There were eight big guns in concrete bunkers, 35 antitank guns in pillboxes, and 85 machine guns, sited to cover three rows of obstacles on the beach below the high-water mark. The four exits from the beach and a belt of shingle, in itself a tank obstacle, had been made more difficult to cross by mines and wire. Within a mile to the rear lay three strong-points, the fortified villages of Colleville sur Mer, St Laurent sur Mer and Vierville sur Mer, giving depth to

RIGHT: *Covered by a smokescreen, landing craft make their final approach to Omaha. Omaha was a much tougher nut to crack than Utah: it had a more complete network of beach defenses and its garrison, units of the German 352nd Division, put up a staunch resistance.*

BELOW: *A DD (Duplex Drive) Sherman lies abandoned on a Normandy beach. During the initial phase of the attack on Omaha, many of these vital weapons were swamped by rough seas after being dropped from their landing craft too far from shore.*

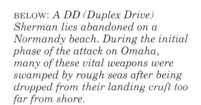

the position. Beyond them was the flooded valley of the River Aure.

The 12-mile run in to Omaha began in darkness and there was no little confusion in the transport area. Landing craft straggled before they crossed the line of departure. Two, carrying the artillery, had actually foundered before reaching the transport areas. Of the 32 DD tanks launched 6000 yards offshore, 27 foundered in the rough seas. Landing craft carried 51 to the shore, but eight of these were knocked out by gunfire. Not less than 10 of the craft carrying infantry were swamped on the run in, and 22 howitzers and an

LEFT: *Smiling US Rangers pictured before their perilous assault on the Pointe du Hoe.*

RIGHT: *Members of the US 1st Infantry Division pose for the camera. This division faced perhaps the toughest test on D-Day.*

FAR RIGHT: *As reinforcements disembark, elements of the first wave begin their advance inland.*

BELOW: *The disposition of the vessels involved in the pre-assault bombardment of the Normandy coast and their main targets.*

BELOW RIGHT: *Crammed into the hold of their transport, US infantry await the order to sail.*

infantry cannon company were lost. The weather was too much for the DUKWs (amphibious trucks), which carried them, and so the infantry struggled ashore without most of the artillery which was supposed to support it, and without tanks.

The Germans held their fire as the assault craft came in. As soon as the first reached the shore, the defenders opened up with a tremendous fire of guns, mortars and machine guns. A landing craft carrying 35 men was hit by four mortar bombs and simply vanished. Men from

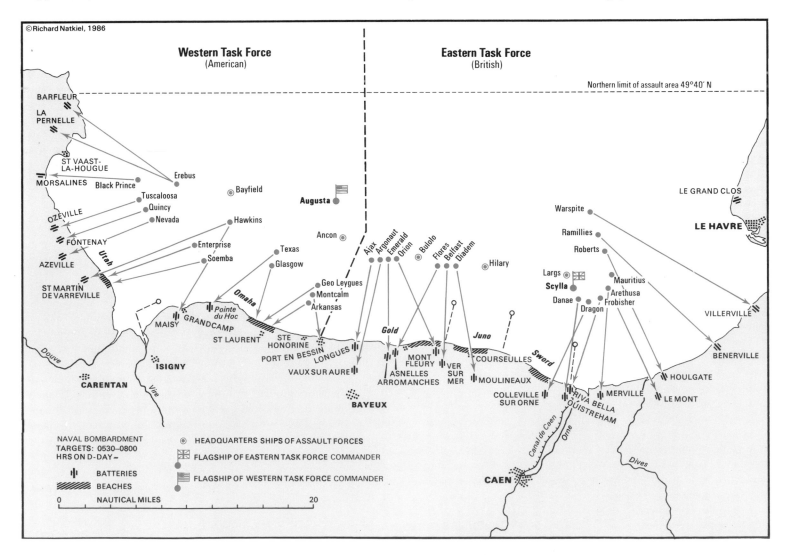

another craft, which foundered 1000 yards offshore, were dragged down by the weight of their equipment. The scattered troops, wading ashore, not always with the units to which they belonged, ran into a hail of bullets and sought such cover as they could find. Some tried to conceal themselves behind the German beach obstacles. Others lay in the water and crept in with the rising tide. Nine companies went into the assault. Two bunched in front of Les Moulins, and elements of four got ashore in the Colleville sector. One company was carried far to the east and landed an hour and a half late. The demolition teams had particularly heavy casualties, much of their equipment was lost and soon the rising tide rendered their work of beach clearance impossible. Only three of the 16 bulldozers allotted to the 116th Infantry got ashore, and one of these was hampered in its movements by exhausted infantry taking cover behind it.

It was not easy for the American observers to make out where their leading troops had got to. The shells of the battleship *Nevada* had shrouded the scene in a cloud of dust!

The follow-up waves came in to find the survivors of the first wave lying at the water's edge or taking cover under the bank of shingle inland of the beach, or at the foot of the bluff. The German fire had not abated. Admiral Hall describes how:

'wave after wave was dispatched from the line of departure close in on the preceding wave, where the combined effect of the wind and tide soon converted the waves into a milling mass in which little semblance of order remained. Had it not been for the appearance on the scene of the Deputy Assault Group Commanders and their prompt action in withdrawing

LEFT: *Covered by the bow-gunner of their landing craft, troops wade ashore at Omaha. Troops pinned down on the shoreline take cover behind a shingle bank; the remains of several halftracks testify to the difficulty of the operation.*

BELOW: *LCIs 553 and 410 land troops of the first assault wave on Omaha partially covered by a smokescreen. LCI 553 was subsequently badly damaged by shellfire and had to be abandoned by its crew.*

and reforming these craft, the success of the entire landing would have been jeopardized.'

It is hardly surprising that the German officer commanding the fortifications at Pointe et Raz de la Percée thought that 'the invasion had been stopped on the beaches.' He could see 10 tanks and a great many other vehicles burning. The defensive fire of his men had been excellent. He could see the dead and wounded lying in the sand. Even so, at about 0730 hours little parties of determined men had begun to struggle through the barbed wire and were working their way inland

through the minefields. Eight United States and three British destroyers gave invaluable fire support at this dangerous period. The tide of battle was turning.

By 0900 hours small groups of American soldiers, which had infiltrated the German posts along the crest, were gradually wiping them out and making their way toward St Laurent and Vierville. Units from 29th and 1st Divisions gathered by Colleville, and with covering fire from a destroyer, had made a gap in the wire and were storming an enemy strongpoint. They had got going again because the officers and non-commissioned officers knew that 'leadership is done from in front.'

ABOVE AND RIGHT: *Two photographs in a sequence of shots depicting the aftermath of accurate German fire off Omaha beach – the survivors of a landing craft are helped ashore by their comrades. Troops were pinned down on the beach for several hours but by 0900 hours scattered groups of GIs had begun to infiltrate through the German defenses.*

LEFT: *Some of the Sherman tanks destined for Omaha beach; few would ever make the shore. Of the 32 tanks launched 6000 yards offshore, 27 foundered in rough seas, while of the 51 carried ashore, eight were almost immediately knocked out by gunfire.*

BELOW: *The dispositions of the rival forces and the Allied objectives on D-Day.*

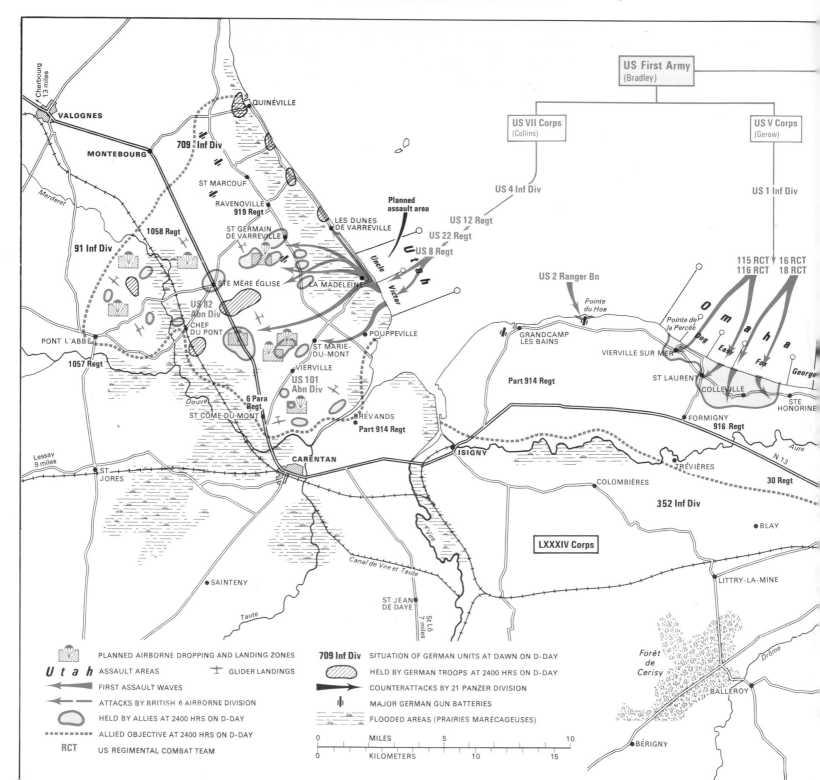

US First Army (Bradley)

US VII Corps (Collins)

US V Corps (Gerow)

US 4 Inf Div

US 1 Inf Div

US 12 Regt

Planned assault area

US 22 Regt

US 8 Regt

US 2 Ranger Bn

115 RCT 16 RCT
116 RCT 18 RCT

709 Inf Div

91 Inf Div

1058 Regt

1057 Regt

919 Regt

US 82 Abn Div

US 101 Abn Div

6 Para Regt

Part 914 Regt

Part 914 Regt

916 Regt

352 Inf Div

30 Regt

LXXXIV Corps

Legend:

- PLANNED AIRBORNE DROPPING AND LANDING ZONES
- *Utah* ASSAULT AREAS
- GLIDER LANDINGS
- FIRST ASSAULT WAVES
- ATTACKS BY BRITISH 6 AIRBORNE DIVISION
- HELD BY ALLIES AT 2400 HRS ON D-DAY
- ALLIED OBJECTIVE AT 2400 HRS ON D-DAY
- RCT US REGIMENTAL COMBAT TEAM
- **709 Inf Div** SITUATION OF GERMAN UNITS AT DAWN ON D-DAY
- HELD BY GERMAN TROOPS AT 2400 HRS ON D-DAY
- COUNTERATTACKS BY 21 PANZER DIVISION
- MAJOR GERMAN GUN BATTERIES
- FLOODED AREAS (PRAIRIES MARÉCAGEUSES)

MILES 0 — 5 — 10
KILOMETERS 0 — 5 — 10 — 15

Map place names: Cherbourg 13 miles, VALOGNES, QUINÉVILLE, MONTEBOURG, ST MARCOUF, Merderet, RAVENOVILLE, ST GERMAIN DE VARREVILLE, LES DUNES DE VARREVILLE, Uncle, Victor, Utah, STE MÈRE ÉGLISE, LA MADELEINE, CHEF DU PONT, PONT L'ABBÉ, ST MARIE-DU-MONT, VIERVILLE, POUPPEVILLE, Douve, ST CÔME-DU-MONT, BRÉVANDS, Lessay 9 miles, ST JORES, CARENTAN, ISIGNY, Canal de Vire et Taute, Vire, SAINTENY, Taute, ST JEAN DE DAYE, St Lô 7 miles, Pointe du Hoe, Pointe de la Percée, GRANDCAMP LES BAINS, VIERVILLE SUR MER, ST LAURENT, COLLEVILLE, STE HONORINE, FORMIGNY, Omaha, Dog, Easy, Fox, George, Aure, TRÉVIÈRES, COLOMBIÈRES, N 13, BLAY, LITTRY-LA-MINE, Forêt de Cerisy, Drôme, BÉRIGNY, BALLEROY

RIGHT: *Dwight Shepler's rendition of the assault on Omaha's Fox Green beach, the objective of elements of the US 16th and 116th Infantry Regiments.*

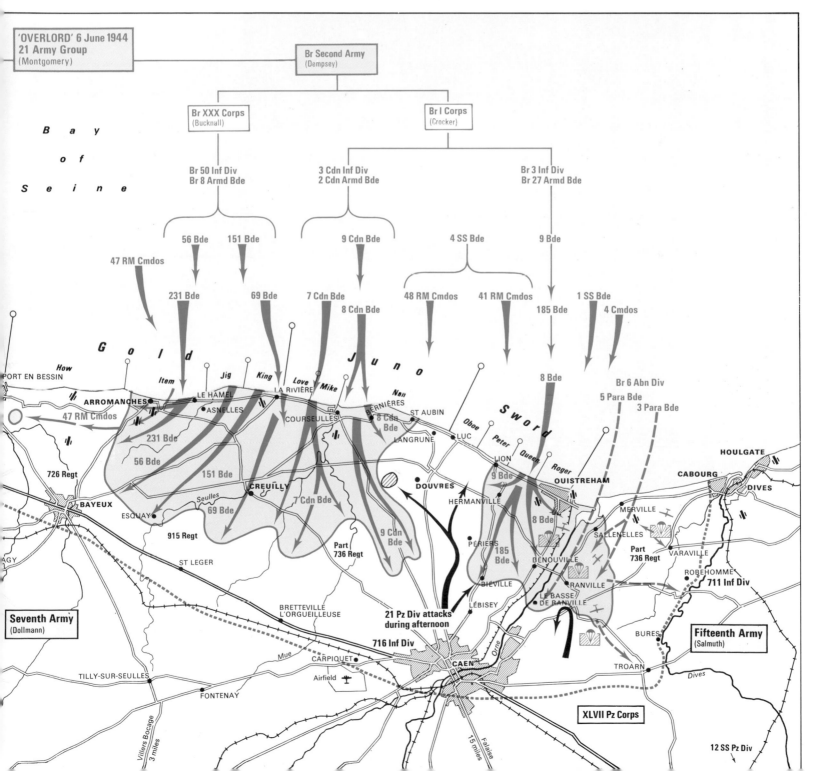

LEFT: *US Rangers enjoy a well-earned rest amid the remains of a German strongpoint on top of the Pointe du Hoe, while German prisoners are escorted into captivity.*

BELOW: *An MP searches German prisoners before they are placed in a temporary compound prior to being transported to prisoner of war camps in England.*

One, who is deservedly remembered, was Colonel Canham, 'They're murdering us here,' he said to men cowering on the beach, 'Let's move inland and get murdered.'

At about 1000 hours Major General C R Huebner, the assault commander, intervened decisively. He held back the waves of vehicles, whose arrival on the beaches could only add to the confusion, and sent in more combat troops. In response to his call for naval gunfire support, destroyers ran in to within 1000 yards of the shore.

A battalion of the 1st Division, veterans of Sicily and Salerno, fought their way through the minefields to attack Colleville. The 29th Division, which was having a very rough time, infiltrated as far as Vierville and St Laurent. About noon the German gunners began to run out of ammunition and, because of the Allied command of the air, convoys could not get through to replenish their supplies.

Meanwhile three companies of US Rangers were carrying out a bold and unusual exploit against the bat-

RIGHT: *The price of victory – one of the 10,300 casualties suffered by the Allies on 6 June.*

tery at Pointe du Hoe. They scaled the cliffs with ropes and ladders and, with covering fire from two destroyers, *Satterlee* (US) and *Talybont* (British), stormed the position only to find that the guns had been removed and concealed inland.

There was a time that morning when a determined counterattack might have driven the US V Corps into the sea. In view of the 352nd Division's optimistic reports, General Marcks sent his reserves elsewhere. By nightfall the Americans had possession of a patch of French soil some six miles long, and in places two miles deep. Reinforcements came in during the night until, with over 34,000 men ashore, the beachhead was secure.

The day's fighting had cost V Corps 3000 casualties, 50 tanks, and 26 guns. In addition 50 landing craft and 10 larger vessels were lost.

The plan for the Omaha landing left much to be desired. However, it was the infantrymen who, despite their top brass, fought and won this vital foothold.

RIGHT: *A US infantryman inspects the remains of a German trench system overlooking Omaha. Taking these positions cost the US V Corps 3000 casualties, 50 tanks and 26 artillery pieces. Naval losses were 50 landing craft and 10 larger vessels.*

5
THE
BRITISH
LANDINGS

The British sector was divided into three assault areas and 10 landing beaches, but the troops went in over only five of them. There were five assault brigades, or rather brigade groups, an intermediate brigade, and four follow-up brigades. In addition there was 1st SS (Special Service) Brigade (Commandos) and 4th SS Brigade (less 46 [RM] Commando).

The 1st Commando Brigade went in on Queen Beach, with the object of joining the 6th Airborne Division as soon as possible, although 4 Commando was first to take Ouistreham.

The 4th Commando Brigade was split up as each unit had a separate task.

	Beach	Task
41 (RM) Cdo	Queen	Capture Lion-sur-Mer
46 (RM) Cdo	—	Capture Houlgate battery
47 (RM) Cdo	Jig	Take Port en Bessin
Bde HQ and 48 (RM) Cdo	Nan	Attack Langrune-sur-Mer

Between Omaha and Gold there was a 10-mile gap. The British sector, between Port en Bessin and the River Orne, stretched for 24 miles.

At midnight on 6 June many of the D-Day objectives, notably Caen were not as yet in British hands. On the other hand the Germans were far from achieving Rommel's aim of driving the invaders straight back into the sea.

Generally speaking, the seaborne landings were successful, which is not to say that everything went according to plan. However, one way and another, and despite the worst a determined enemy could do, every group managed sooner or later to carry out its task.

The most westerly objective of any British unit was Port en Bessin, the inter-Allied boundary. This was to be attacked by 47 (RM) Commando. They had a rough landing on Gold Beach near St Côme de Fresne as the majority of their 16 landing craft were hit. As the first wave waded ashore it came under such heavy machine-gun fire that one marine is said to have remarked, 'Perhaps we're intruding. This seems to be a private beach.' The commando suffered 43 casualties in the landing. The rest concentrated at the back of the beach, and then set off westward across country. It had a sharp fight at La Rosière in the evening, but eventually reached Point 72, a prominent hill 1.5 miles south of its objective, where the marines dug in for the night. They attacked the little town of Port en Bessin next day, and with some fire support from HMS *Emerald* and three squadrons of rocket-firing Typhoons gradually overcame the opposition, though with heavy casualties. Eventually at 0400 hours on 8 June, the garrison, still 300 strong, surrendered. The little harbor was put to immediate use, and proved of great value.

The 231st Brigade, veterans of the invasion of Sicily, landed on a two-battalion front. On their front the fortified village of Le Hamel was the main German strongpoint. This was still holding when the second wave went in at about 0815 hours, and began to press toward Arromanches les Bains. The 1st Hampshires, the right

PREVIOUS PAGES: *Landing craft carrying members of the 1st Special Service Brigade close on the village of Ouistreham, an objective lying on the Roger section of Sword beach.*

LEFT: *Men of the British 50th Division, part of XXX Corps, come ashore on Gold beach, the most westerly of the British landings. These troops were tasked with effecting a link up with the US forces pushing inland from Omaha and securing the harbor facilities at Port en Bessin.*

RIGHT: *British commandos and an airborne liaison officer (second from right) come ashore amid the wreckage of an earlier assault wave.*

assault battalion, lost its senior officers and progress was slow and costly. However the 1st Dorsets took Les Roquettes and pushed inland. Flail tanks of the Westminster Dragoons and other 'Funnies' landed punctually and set to work clearing mines and obstacles.

The 6th Battalion, Green Howards, of 69th Brigade made short work of a strongpoint at Hable de Heurtot and a battery position at Mont Fleury, whose gunners had been discouraged by bombing and by 12 direct hits from HMS *Orion*. In this fighting Sergeant Major S E Hollis won the Victoria Cross.

At La Rivière the 5th Battalion, East Yorks, was cornered by the sea wall, but naval gunfire and a flail tank from the Westminster Dragoons solved the problem. The tank knocked out an 88mm gun in its bunker and 45 prisoners were taken. There followed a long, hard fight for the village, which cost 90 casualties. Two guns and 30 prisoners were taken in the strongpoint at the lighthouse near Mont Fleury. The battalion then pushed on inland toward Ver sur Mer. The 7th Battalion, Green Howards, passed through the assault battalions and took a battery beyond that village. It had been softened up by bombing and by HMS *Belfast*, and yielded 50 gunners, who had fired 87 rounds from their four 10cm howitzers before losing heart.

The two assault brigade groups of the 50th Division, supported by DD tanks of the 4/7th Dragoon Guards and the Nottinghamshire Yeomanry were now pushing inland, and at about 1100 hours the 151st Brigade began to land over the beaches taken by the 69th Brigade. Le

RIGHT: *British commandos move inland, heading for elements of the 6th Airborne Division to the east of the River Orne.*

Hamel was still holding out, but by the early afternoon all four brigades of 50th Division were ashore. Since the oft-rehearsed counterattack of the 915th German Infantry Regiment did not come to pass, progress was fairly satisfactory, although the 56th Brigade met with opposition outside Bayeux, which, however, fell next day.

The 3rd Canadian Division Group, which had not been in action before, landed a little late due to the rough weather. Most of its DD tanks got ashore, some of them ahead of the infantry. Effective covering fire from destroyers and support craft kept the Germans quiet until the landing craft touched down. The crews behaved with great resolution and valor, driving the larger landing craft on to the shore, and worming the smaller ones through the numerous obstacles as best they could. Ninety out of 306 landing craft employed by Force J were lost or damaged.

Courseulles, one of the main German positions on the Canadian front, held out stubbornly against the Regina Rifles, and there was fierce street fighting until well into the afternoon.

The Winnipeg Rifles, the reserve battalion of the 7th Canadian Brigade, avoided Courseulles and made good progress. They took Vaux and Ste Croix sur Mer.

Bernières, like Courseulles, was a hard nut to crack. The sea wall was 12 feet high in places, and behind it there were many fortified houses. Some had been demolished by naval gunfire, but the strongpoint was still a formidable one. Its infantry garrison had the support of two 50mm antitank guns, two heavy mortars and eight machine guns. The Queen's Own Rifles were enfiladed as they dashed across the beach, and suffered heavy losses. However, once they had outflanked the position by storming the sea wall, the defenders gave up. St Aubin sur Mer held out for three hours against the North Shore Regiment and assault engineers' tanks, and sniping went on until night fell.

By 1400 hours the whole Canadian division was ashore: infantry, artillery and armor. The narrow strip of beach, slowly being covered by the rising tide, was choked with troops and vehicles, while damaged landing craft littered the water's edge. Congestion on the beaches, and in Bernières, delayed the Canadians. When they tried to debouch into the open, undulating country beyond they were met by the fire of 88s and machine guns. Between Rivière and Bernières there were 11 antitank guns, belonging to the 716th Division, disposed across the path of the Canadians within a mile of the coast. Even so the 7th Canadian Brigade made

ABOVE LEFT: *A Hawker Typhoon, perhaps the most successful British ground-attack aircraft of the war, patrols the skies over the Normandy beaches. Their strafing attacks did much to delay the arrival of German armored formations at the invasion front.*

LEFT: *British troops, including a member of the 50th Division (left) examine the remains of a concrete artillery emplacement. The 50th Division was landed on Gold and had to fight hard to clear the village of Le Hamel of its German garrison.*

good progress, taking Banville and Ste Croix sur Mer, and 'hordes of prisoners.' By 1600 hours they were across the Seulles. Three companies of the 726th Infantry Regiment had departed in disorder at their approach.

Near Fontaine-Henry the Regina Rifles, supported by tanks, came under heavy fire from 88s, but pushed on and took Le Fresne-Camilly.

The 8th Canadian Brigade took a battery 1000 yards west of Tailleville, bypassing another with 80 rockets, whose cables had been cut by the bombing so that they could not be fired. By 1430 hours, Bény sur Mer had fallen with 50 prisoners and a battery of the 171th Artillery Regiment (four 10cm guns) which had received more than 200 5.25-inch shells from HMS *Diadem*. At Tailleville a battalion HQ with a company of the 736th Grenadier Regiment held out in fortified houses connected by tunnels.

Thus the two leading Canadian brigades had advanced four or five miles inland. By 1430 hours the reserve brigade (9th) had made its way through Bernières and assembled south of the town. Its objective was Carpiquet, 10 miles away. It was not until after 1900 hours that the brigade reached Bèny sur Mer, though some of the North Nova Scotia Highlanders, lifted on tanks of the 27th Canadian Armored Regiment, arrived in the dusk at Villons les Buissons, after capturing some mortars and antitank guns. There was German armor, from 21st Panzer, between this force and the British 3rd Division. The Canadians were ordered to form a 'fortress' round the crossroads, where the road from Anisy to Villons les Buissons crosses that from Courseulles to Caen.

ABOVE: *Elements of the Canadian 3rd Division land on Juno beach. One of the division's objectives, the village of Courseulles, held out until mid-afternoon, but elsewhere the Canadians made steady progress.*

RIGHT: *Canadian troops dig in on Juno. In the foreground several wounded await evacuation from the beachhead.*

LEFT: *With Omaha beach secure, US troops move forward to link up with the British forces advancing on Port en Bessin. The town and its garrison finally surrendered at 0400 hours on 8 June after heavy fighting.*

BELOW: *Dejected German prisoners are escorted to the rear by members of the 13th/18th Hussars. This armored regiment lost 10 of its tanks during the initial approach to Sword beach, leaving 28 to support units of the 3rd Division.*

Considering the congestion at Bernières the inexperienced but hardy Canadians did rather well on D-Day, though it is true that they were not counterattacked. Their armor had been particularly successful, knocking out a dozen or more of the dreaded 88s. Two troops of the 1st Hussars had actually reached the objective, the Bayeux-Caen road. However, they lacked infantry support and were compelled to fall back to their squadron.

The HQ of the 4th SS Brigade and 48 Commando encountered the difficulties landing on Nan Beach (Juno) at about 0900 hours. Five of their six landing craft struck mines and one was hit by shellfire; two of them sank. A 'heavy swell and a vicious tidal stream . . . carried away and drowned men attempting to swim.' The beach defenses had survived the preliminary bombardment, but with the cover of a smoke screen the commandos reached the cover of a low cliff and the sea wall, to find themselves among:

'a jumble of men from other units, including many wounded and dead; the beach was congested with tanks, heavy propelled guns and other vehicles . . . Tank landing craft were arriving all the time and attempting to land their loads, added to the general confusion.'

Y Troop, whose officers had become casualties, were taken back to England by a tank landing craft which had picked it up when its own craft had sunk. It was unable to rejoin its unit until two weeks later. Z Troop, some 40 strong, landed thanks to a stout-hearted leading seaman, who ferried the men ashore in two lifts.

No 48 Commando, now only some 200 strong, took Langrune but was then held by a strongpoint near the shore. With the aid of a Sherman tank this was taken at about 1600 hours on 7 June. Two officers and 33 men of the 736th Grenadier Regiment laid down their arms. They had made a very credible defense.

The 3rd Division, which Montgomery had commanded in the Dunkirk campaign, was the one with which he had first made his name. He never concealed his view that it was much better trained than the others in the BEF, and it had certainly proved itself a very useful formation. It must be said, however, that it was not really any better than other divisions, for example 1st and 4th, whose commanders were disinclined to publicize their exploits.

Since 1940 the 3rd Division had spent four years

RIGHT: *Commandos head down a French road, moving inland in an attempt to secure their D-Day objectives. No Allied unit was able to reach the perhaps overly ambitious targets set by the operation's planners.*

BELOW RIGHT: *Heavily laden commandos wade through knee-high surf to reach one of the invasion beaches. DD Shermans, with their flotation 'skirts' folded, are dotted along the shoreline.*

training in England, without any taste of active service. That it was thoroughly trained will be obvious. It may be that it had reached, and indeed passed, the point when it was overtrained. It is possible, though this is not a criticism which can be applied to *all* units of the division, that it was a bit 'stale.'

The British 3rd Division, under Major General T G Rennie, was to attack on a front of one brigade. It landed on Queen Beach and spread out to cover the 2.5 miles between Lion sur Mer and Ouistreham. Both places were well fortified and about halfway between them was a strongpoint at La Brèche, bristling with wire, machine guns, mortars and the usual guns in casemates. The countryside was flat. On the north side of the coast road was a fairly high ridge of sand crowned with a more or less continuous row of houses.

The 8th Brigade landed on time and in the right place. Fire support was effective, but as the craft neared the shore the Germans opened up. Most of the DD tanks of the 13th/18th Hussars were launched at sea, and though 10 were knocked out in the surf, or soon after, 28 were left to support the infantry. The armored vehicles of the assault engineers landed with the leading wave and were the only supporting troops available from the very outset.

Here as elsewhere the crews of the landing craft showed the utmost determination. Of 18 craft that carried the self-propelled guns of the 7th, 33rd and 76th Field Regiments, Royal Artillery, 14 became total wrecks; five from the effects of obstacles, three from mines and six from enemy fire. Miraculous though it may seem the 20 landing craft carrying the first infantry wave of 8th Brigade all got ashore without a casualty at 0730 hours. The leading companies of 1st South Lancashire and 2nd East Yorkshire Regiments began to attack the La Brèche strongpoint and to clear the houses along the dunes. 41 (RM) Commando (4th SS

Brigade), which suffered heavy casualties on the beach, set off to attack Lion sur Mer. It made some progress, but the place was not finally subdued until next day, when a battalion of the Lincolnshire Regiment attacked it.

Along with two French troops of 10 (Inter-Allied) Commando, 4 Commando landed at 0820 hours on the heels of 8th Brigade, which they found 'pinned to the beach by intense fire.' The commando passed through them, and took a pillbox which had been causing casualties. Then, led by the French troops under Commandant Kieffer, they moved against the defenses of Ouistreham. A French gendarme, who met them, rendered invaluable service, by pointing out the various German positions. After severe hand-to-hand fighting 4 Commando, with the support of four Centaur tanks

from the Royal Marine Armored Support Regiment, took the Riva Bella battery, though not without heavy casualties.

A superb unit, 6 Commando, set off to blaze a trail inland and join hands with the 6th Airborne at the Bénouville bridge. 3 and 45 (RM) Commandos were to go in at H+90 and to follow 6 Commando. With the exception of 45 Commando, which was going into action for the first time, the 1st Commando Brigade was rather more experienced than most of the Allied troops who landed on D-Day. 4 Commando had stormed the Varengeville battery at Dieppe, 6 Commando had fought with great distinction in North Africa, and 3 had been at Vaagso, Dieppe, and the landings in Sicily and Italy.

Neither the La Brèche strongpoint nor Ouistreham had been subdued when at about 0900 hours the five

landing craft infantry (LCI) carrying 3 Commando arrived 1000 yards from the beach and hove to within easy range of quite a number of German guns. They formed a line abreast with the precision worthy of a ceremonial parade.

The author of this book was commanding 3 Commando on this occasion. I was on the bridge of a landing craft talking to Lieutenant P Whitworth who commanded our division. The sea ran high, the weather was dull and gloomy, but the sight of HMS *Ramillies* belching 15-inch shells at the Bénerville battery was almost as good as a rum ration. A shell landed in the water 100 yards away and to port we could see a tank landing craft blazing; the crew was going over the side as the ammunition exploded. Battered houses along the shore looked vaguely familiar from the photographs we had been shown. Tanks were creeping about on the beach, but from in front of Ouistreham a German gun was firing at us every few seconds. This did not seem to be the time or the place to slow down. I asked Lieutenant Whitworth what he was waiting for.

'There are still five minutes to go before H+90,' he said with admirable sang froid.

'I don't think anyone will mind,' I replied, 'if we're five minutes *early* on D-Day.'

'Then in we go.'

We set off in a beautiful line, and not a moment too soon. Another shell. An airburst just ahead; the bits that reached us had lost all force. Then the next craft to starboard was hit, and seem to shy like a horse. As we beached the gun at Ouistreham hit us and many of my men were up to their necks in water before they could struggle out of the hold.

The 4th division got all its five craft ashore, though three were hit and two completely wrecked. Such was the spirit of the RNVR, who put us ashore on D-Day. The commando lost about 30 men, mostly from the explosion of our own mortar bombs in one of the striken

ABOVE LEFT: *Despite the strenuous effort of his comrades to keep the gangplank secure, a Royal Marine commando, encumbered by a bicycle, tumbles into the sea.*

LEFT: *Members of the 1st Special Service Brigade's Signal Troop move inland. In the background is a Churchill bridge-layer, used to help cross both natural and manmade obstacles.*

RIGHT: LST 21 *unloads tanks and trucks onto a 'Rhino' barge as the race to rush reinforcements to the Normandy bridgehead begins.*

BELOW RIGHT: *The* Evening Despatch *announces the progress of Operation Overlord to the British public.*

craft. The first man ashore was Major J E Martin, our veteran administrative officer, who, as a trooper in the 9th Lancers, had had his baptism of fire on the Western Front in the year that I was born. He went right through – from Normandy to the Baltic.

There were quite a lot of infantry sitting about on the beach, and one cried out, 'Don't touch the bloody wire, it's mined.' We sorted ourselves out among the houses on the dunes, undisturbed except for a little indiscriminate mortar fire. Ahead lay 1000 yards of flat marshy meadow without a vestige of cover.

This, the first stage of our journey to the Bénouville bridges, was covered by a German quick-firing gun, but we survived its attentions more or less unscathed and pushed on to our forming-up place. Nearby we found a company commander of the assault brigade. He had his CSM (Company Sergeant Major) and two men with him. The rest, I rather thought, might be the men we had seen sitting on the beach.

La Brèche fell at about 1000 hours, after causing the assault brigade heavy casualties. The beaches were still under fire from guns inland, some of them beyond the Orne, but the 185th and 9th Brigades were able to come ashore during the morning and early afternoon. During the morning the 8th Brigade took Hermanville and Colleville and attacked two strongpoints, Morris and Hillman, a mile beyond. The first, which had suffered from air and naval bombardment, surrendered with 67 men and four field guns as soon as the attack began. The second, which was the well-sited HQ of the 736th Regiment, held out until 2000 hours.

By about 1000 hours the infantry of 185th Brigade Group had assembled in woods about half a mile inland. Its vehicles and heavy weapons, however, were held up by congestion on the beaches and by minefields. So at about 1230 hours the foot soldiers set off without them, reaching Périers ridge at about 1400 hours. Here they were joined by the leading tanks of the Staffordshire Yeomanry. There were German guns in the woods to their right, and these knocked out five tanks. They had to be ejected. The Staffordshires occupied a feature

called Point 61, as a flank guard and base of fire, and the rest of the column moved on in the direction of Caen. It was some hours before the main body of the brigade got going. At 1500 hours 1st Battalion, Royal Norfolks, was ordered to secure high ground on the left of 2nd Battalion, King's Shropshire Light Infantry. They thought St Aubin d'Arquenay was still in German hands, though

in fact the commando brigade – including the present writer – went through it about noon, making for Bénouville. Under this misapprehension the Norfolks moved through a large field, where, sadly they soon lost 150 casualties to the machine guns of Hillman. It was not until 1900 hours that Beauville and Biéville were in British hands. The 2nd Battalion, Royal Warwickshires, ordered to advance late in the afternoon, occupied St Aubin d'Arquenay at about 1800 hours – at least six hours after the commandos had passed through. Opinions will differ as to whether this lack of urgency should be attributed to brigade or battalion.

Hesitation, at the highest level, afflicted the opposition. At 1432 hours Army Group B at last received permission – 12 hours after it had been requested – to move up 12th SS Panzer in support of Seventh Army. At 1507 hours authority was received to move I SS Panzer Corps and Panzer *Lehr* Division. General Dollmann (Seventh Army) ordered Lieutenant General Bayerlein (Panzer *Lehr*) to move on Caen at 1700 hours. The latter, with memories of the RAF in the Western Desert, urged that it was foolish to move before nightfall, but Dollmann, determined to attack at dawn on 7 July, would have none of this. Before Bayerlein and his HQ had passed Beaumont sur Sarthe the bombs began to fall. A nightmare move followed, with Allied aircraft striking at every bottleneck on the five routes by which the long columns of vehicles were struggling to advance. Bayerlein wrote:

'At 2300 we drove through Sées. The place was lit up by flares hanging above it like candles on a Christmas tree, and heavy bombs were crashing down on the houses which were already burning. But we managed to get through.'

Meanwhile Feuchtinger had made his counterattack against 3rd Division. Under the continuous air attack requested by Dempsey, the 21st Panzer had crossed the Orne. By this time the 8th Brigade at Hermanville, Colleville sur Orne and Ouistreham was fairly well set, though 2nd Battalion, East Yorkshires, was occupied with a battery (Daimler) south of Ouistreham, and 1st Battalion, Suffolks, with the Hillman strongpoint. The 9th Brigade was assembling just inland of the beach, but was not yet ready to advance into the gap between the Canadians and Hermanville. The main body of the 185th Brigade was moving on Caen. The 2nd Battalion, King's Shropshire Light Infantry (KSLI) with a squadron of tanks (Staffordshire Yeomanry) and some anti-tank guns, was at Beauville and Biéville. It must be said that KSLI seems to have had a real sense of the need to thrust forward on D-Day.

Soon after 1600 hours German tanks were reported moving up from Caen. A squadron supporting 1st Battalion, Suffolks, at Hillman was immediately moved to Biéville. No sooner had it taken up its position than 40 German tanks, moving very fast, came in from the west. The Staffordshire Yeomanry knocked out two with their 6-pounders. The rest sheared off into the woods. When they reappeared they suffered more casualties. Veering off once more, they were reinforced, and working round the right (western) flank approached the Périers bridge. They ran into the squadron which had been positioned at Point 61 for just such an eventuality. The Germans lost three more tanks, and once again retired. They were now known by the British to have lost 13 tanks at a cost of one self-propelled gun. In fact Feuchtinger's losses were much heavier. According to him he began the day with 124 tanks, of which 54 were

RIGHT: *British trucks are checked by their drivers before heading inland with their cargoes of supplies for the troops fighting at the front.*

BELOW LEFT: *Watched over by a beachmaster (center), landing craft discharge their cargoes. Note the metal roadway, designed to overcome the difficulties of crossing soft sand.*

BELOW RIGHT: *British troops survey the wreckage of a German flak ship sunk in the harbor of Port en Bessin, 13 June.*

knocked out by nightfall. Eight Typhoons of the Second Tactical Air Force had accounted for six by dive bombing them on the outskirts of Caen. The division was nearly out of gasoline.

The repulse of 21st Panzer is very much to the credit of 3rd Division, and if they may be criticized for slowness, they deserve credit for their staunch conduct in the face of this dangerous counterattack.

The commando brigade joined hands with the 6th Airborne Division at about midday, the first commandos arriving on folding cycles. Lovat sent them with all speed to relieve 9th Parachute Battalion and secure the Amfreville-Le Plein ridge, which overlooked the 3rd Division's area.

'We reached the bridges to find that they were under a desultory fire from a building perhaps 800 yards to the south. A group belonging to my bicycle troop were taking cover under the low bank to the left of the road.

I told them to get on their bikes and go across flat out. One was shot clean through the head. The rest got through. Now it was our turn, and we showed a very pretty turn of speed.

Lord Lovat came up, and told me that our planned move to Cabourg was off. We were to occupy Le Bas de Ranville so as to protect the HQ of the 6th Airborne Division and to block the German armor coming from the south. As we have seen the 21 Panzer did not turn up, which was just as well for we had not much in the way of antitank weapons. So we passed a peaceful afternoon in the June sunshine.'

At about 2100 hours some 240 gliders towed by transport aircraft, came flying in low over the coast to land at Bénouville and Ranville. It was an astonishing sight. At a stroke the effective strength of the 6th Airborne Division was doubled. The reinforcements included two strong battalions and the reconnaissance regiment as well as some artillery. The effect on the morale of both sides was marked.

The telephone log of the German Seventh Army records, 'Attack by the 21st Panzer Division rendered useless by heavily concentrated airborne troops.' Rommel's HQ was told that the 21st Panzer had 'been halted by renewed air landings.' The sight of this massed air landing taking place in their rear was naturally very

discouraging to the Germans and led them to call off their counterattack. The panzers fell back to a position between the KSLI and Caen. At midnight Seventh Army's signals diary summed up the situation in the Caen area:

'2400 hours. 716th Infantry Division is still defending itself at strongpoints. Communications between division, regimental and battalion headquarters, however, no longer exist, so that nothing is known as to the number of strongpoints still holding out or those liquidated. . . . The Chief of Staff of Seventh Army gives the order that the counterattack of 7 June must reach the coast without fail, since the strongpoint defenders expect it of us.'

They were due for a disappointment.

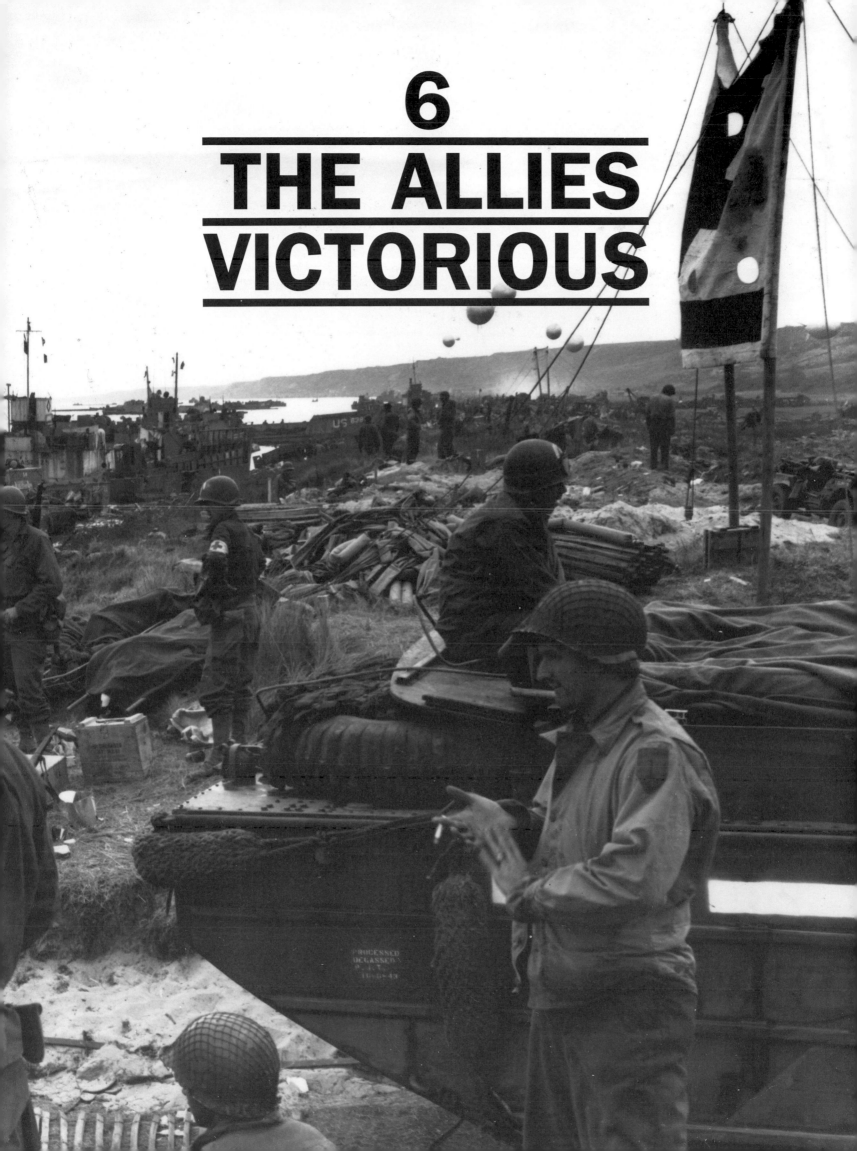

6
THE ALLIES
VICTORIOUS

Why did the Allies win the battle on D-Day? Was Montgomery a greater general than von Rundstedt? Why did the Germans, with some 40 divisions at their disposal, get so many of them in the wrong places that the Allies were able to fight their way ashore, and stay there?

It must be remembered that in the first place the Allies had complete command in the air. In the second they had absolute command at sea. In the third, though Montgomery was not without fault he was probably a much better general than von Rundstedt, besides being more than a match for Rommel. He was, moreover, nobly supported by Bradley and Dempsey.

If the Allies had the advantage in the air and at sea, the Germans should have had a tremendous advantage on land, for they had far more divisions and, especially, many more panzer divisions. Moreover their men were, on the whole, much more experienced than the Allies'. They were well led at every level.

The key point is that for one reason or another the German commanders were in two minds as to the significance of the reports that reached their headquarters. At 0215 hours Major General Pemsel reported to Rommel's Chief of Staff, General Speidel, 'the sound of engines can be heard coming from the sea on the eastern Cotentin coast . . . ,' and that Admiral, Channel Coast, reported the presence of ships in the sea off Cherbourg. To Pemsel all this activity indicated a major operation. Speidel did not agree and, more to the point, nor did von Rundstedt, who remained convinced that the main attack must come at Calais, and that therefore it had not yet begun.

Von Rundstedt was the key figure in the crisis, for Rommel was away. Keitel's opinion was neither here not there, for had von Rundstedt been convinced that the genuine D-Day had arrived, one may suppose that

the old Prussian warrior would have used his initiative and moved his reserves to where he thought Montgomery would least like to see them.

The most effective place to attack was Caen. A strong counterattack against the British left flank was the Germans' best chance of doing real damage on D-Day. As the campaign developed Montgomery expressed himself as being very well content to hold the mass of the German armor on the British front. However that may have been later on, a mass of German armor round Caen was the last thing the British wanted to meet on D-Day. Thanks to von Rundstedt's initial misapprehension there was only one panzer division near enough to make itself felt early in the day. This was 21st Panzer under Lieutenant General Edgar Feuchtinger, an officer by no means lacking in initiative. His division was stationed at St Pierre sur Dives, only 15 miles from the coast. He had some 170 armored vehicles and tanks at his command. He has described the frustrations he suffered during the early hours of 6 June:

'I waited impatiently all night for some instructions. But not a single order from a higher formation was received by me. Realizing that my armored division was closest to the scene of operations, I finally decided at 0630 hours that I had to take some action. I ordered my tanks to attack the 6th Airborne Division which had entrenched itself in a bridgehead over the Orne. To me this constituted the most immediate threat to the German position.'

This was a shrewd and correct judgment, the more so as the 6th Airborne was very far from being entrenched by 0630, nor had it yet been reinforced by the commandos. Feuchtinger continues:

'Hardly had I made this decision when at 0700 hours I received my first intimation that a higher command did still

PREVIOUS PAGES: *A picture taken shortly after Omaha beach was made secure. The chaos on the shoreline, the dead and wounded, and the tiredness of the troops testify to the tough nature of the fighting.*

LEFT: *Twenty-four hours after D-Day US troops prepare one of the invasion beaches for the arrival of reinforcements and supplies.*

RIGHT: *Watched over by an antiaircraft gun (left foreground), US trucks leave one of the invasion beaches.*

exist. I was told by Army Group B that I was now under command of Seventh Army. But I received no further orders as to my role.

At 0900 hours I was informed that I would receive any future orders from LXXXIV Infantry Corps (Marcks), and finally at 1000 hours I was given my first operational instructions. I was ordered to stop the move of my tanks against the Allied airborne troops, and to turn west and aid the forces protecting Caen.'

This was the crucial decision. Feuchtinger's armor, which had already been moving toward the coast 90 minutes before the first man of the British 3rd Division set foot ashore, was now condemned to spend the vital hours of D-Day in recrossing the single surviving bridge over the Orne at Caen. Had it carried out its original plan the 21st Panzer must have advanced via La Bas de Ranville, which was held that afternoon by 3

RIGHT: *With the beaches secure, the Allies were able to pour war materials into the Normandy bridgehead. Both the Luftwaffe and Kriegsmarine were unable to halt the flow of supplies.*

LEFT: *Three of the senior officers involved in Operation Overlord inspect one of the invasion beaches: General Omar Bradley (right); Rear Admiral Hall (third from right); and Rear Admiral Kirk (second from left).*

Commando under the present author. An unpleasant situation would have occurred.

Another German commander who reacted quickly was General F Dollmann, the commander of the Seventh Army. In the early hours of 6 June he gave orders for a three-pronged attack which, coming in from north, south and west, would crush the American airborne divisions. Unfortunately for him, his divisional commanders had not got back from Rennes, where they had been attending an anti-invasion exercise. American soldiers and Resistance fighters alike had

been busy cutting telephone lines, and several German commanders were simply unable to communicate with their headquarters. Chaos and darkness were their lot, and that of their subordinates.

One of the best units in the Cotentin was the 6th German Parachute Regiment. It was decided to use it for the attack on the Americans between Carentan and Ste Mère Eglise, which has already been mentioned. Major Friedrich-August Freiherr von der Heydte collected his men, and then surveyed the scene from the tower of St Côme church. Six miles away he could see Utah, and

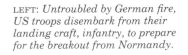

LEFT: *Untroubled by German fire, US troops disembark from their landing craft, infantry, to prepare for the breakout from Normandy.*

RIGHT AND FAR RIGHT: *Supplies come ashore at Port en Bessin.*

found the sight 'overwhelming.' There, in the middle of the morning of D-Day, scores of landing craft were peacefully unloading in the sunshine. It was like 'Berlin Wannsee on a summer's afternoon.' The American airborne troops reported in the area were nowhere to be seen.

Von der Heydte's first battalion broke through the scattered units of 101st Division without any difficulty, but his unit was cut in two by a follow-up landing of gliders and paratroops. The advance of US 8th Infantry Division from Utah spelled disaster for the 6th German Parachute Regiment, but they were not to know that until next day, 7 June.

At Omaha General Dietrich Kraiss, as we have seen, was convinced that his 352nd Division had stopped the Americans in their tracks. Reports from 716th Division were not so encouraging. The British were pressing toward Bayeux, where LXXXIV Corp's reserve, 915th Regiment, was stationed. This unit had practised the counterattack toward the coast not once but many times. Now was the time to carry it out in earnest. Imagine Kraiss' wrath when, at 0400 hours, he discovered that the 915th Regiment had been sent up to Carentan to mop up the airborne landing! The general's reaction was to send a counterorder, which took an hour to get through. The troops – one may imagine their comments – turned about and moving on foot, on bicycles and in old French *camions* moved toward Omaha. However, one way and another they never managed to reinforce the defenders, who were gradually being winkled out of their bunkers. A veritable curtain of naval gunfire did much to prevent the replenishment of ammunition, which was essential if the Germans in the front line were to hold out. The counterattack of 915th Regiment came to nothing. A rather more dangerous onslaught was made by the 21st Panzer which, hampered by refugees, had made its way through Caen. The Allies were already in sight of the city with its tall cathedral when, late in the afternoon General Feuchtinger sent his armor in. He wrote:

'Once over the Orne river I drove north toward the coast. By this time the enemy . . . had made astonishing progress and had already occupied a strip of high ground about 10 kilometers from the sea. From here, the excellent antitank gunfire of the Allies knocked out 11 of my tanks before I had barely started. However, one battle group did manage to bypass these guns and actually reached the coast at Lion sur Mer, at about 1900 hours.'

This force, half a dozen tanks and a handful of infantry, was insufficient to turn the tide of battle. Indeed about three hours earlier the British had come up against the last tanks of the 21st Panzer counterattacking to save Caen. Before the Germans went into the attack General Marcks, with all the gravity he could muster, told their battalion commander, Colonel von Oppeln-Bronowski:

'Oppeln, the future of Germany may very well rest on your shoulders. If you don't push the British back we've lost the war.'

Nobody, who has not fought with and beaten the Germans, need trouble to boast of his soldiership! Yet for once these war-wise warriors were taken by surprise. Rommel, for one, had been on leave. The storm in the Channel put the Germans off their guard. None of these things would have mattered had von Rundstedt's initial dispositions been correct. The Germans had a long tradition of expertise in land operations but von Rundstedt proved incapable of countering an amphibious operation. He should have seen that there were only two areas where the Allies could make their initial landfall. The obvious one was the Pas de Calais; the other was the one actually chosen, the area between the Orne and the Cotentin. A combination of the two, though unlikely, was possible. It follows that the infantry in each of these areas should have been good quality, mobile divisions. Low grade static divisions were simply not good enough. In addition each of these two vital areas needed at least *two* panzer divisions, one on each flank, and a corps reserve of at least one more well-trained infantry division.

LEFT: *An aerial view of one of the Allied Mulberry harbors at Arromanches. Although badly damaged by storms on 19 June, these safe anchorages greatly aided the flow of equipment to the troops in the field.*

BELOW LEFT: *British troops supported by a Sherman tank move through the village of Reviers during the drive on Caen.*

Field Marshal von Rundstedt, for all his service and experience, was baffled by the complexities of amphibious warfare. Even so it should not have been beyond his wit to work out that some parts of the coast were simply not going to be included in the Allies' beachhead area. One was the stretch of coast on either side of Dieppe, with its steep chalk cliffs and shingle beaches – especially after the fiasco of 1942. It follows that in this area the 84th Field Division could have been replaced by a low-category static formation. Another area which was held with unnecessary strength was Brittany. There was no need for the 77th Division at St Malo, which could have been replaced by a static garrison. The same applies to the 353rd Division as an Allied landing in Brittany was highly improbable. Not only was it much farther from the ports of the south of England, it was too far from Paris, Antwerp and the other main objectives of any Allied campaign. Had von Rundstedt analyzed the situation more astutely and made a sounder allocation of his best divisions, it is possible that the Allies would have been repulsed on D-Day.

The D-Day battle fell naturally into three phases. The first was the breaking of the Atlantic Wall, the second was the thrust inland, and the third was the consolidation in order to repel the inevitable counterattack.

The first phase, despite initial setbacks at Omaha, was everywhere remarkably successful. The Atlantic Wall, for all the skill that had gone into its construction, proved a great deal less formidable than expected. Or, to put in another way, the Allied troops, and particularly the British and Canadians, came trained and equipped to deal with every sort of obstacle. This is perhaps the place to pay tribute to Major General Sir Percy Hobart, whose 'funny' tanks loaded the dice in favor of the British infantryman.

Progress made in the second phase of the D-Day fighting was disappointing, in that Caen, Bayeux and Carentan were still in German hands when night fell. It must be remembered that the planners were bound to be optimistic in selecting their objectives for D-Day. Complete success was not perhaps to be looked for from troops who, after a night spent being seasick in ships and landing craft, had already stormed the West Wall. Credit must go to those, including 6th Airborne and the commandos, who actually attained their objectives.

In any big amphibious operation it is essential at the outset to capture enough ground to give the force room to maneuver. Experience shows that one can capture terrain on D-Day which thereafter can only be taken at heavy cost, because the enemy has had time to organize defenses. It therefore behoves the advancing troops to take risks on D-Day, to get a move on. It cannot be said that all the Allied troops engaged bore this is mind. Some, it must be said, were decidedly cautious. It was rather unfortunate for the British that the 21st Panzer appeared on the front of a division which had been trained to plod forward at 100 yards in three minutes, covered by massive artillery fire. Tactics appropriate enough for a set-piece battle were not necessarily the best answer for the fluid situation met with on D-Day.

The consolidation phase was something which the Allied commanders at every level thoroughly understood. They were quick to dig in and secure the ground they had gained. Thanks to such imaginative devices as the Mulberry harbor and PLUTO (Pipeline Under The

RIGHT: *An abandoned DD Sherman, formerly attached to the British 3rd Division, lies in one of the airborne landing zones.*

Ocean) the administrative buildup put the army group on a sound footing in good time before, on 19 June, the worst storm in the Channel for more than 40 years struck the assault area.

Many years have passed since the Allies won this astonishing victory. It is not likely that the world will see such another, for a single nuclear weapon in the assault area might suffice to bring the whole amphibious machine to a disastrous halt. It is a solemn thought.

Yet, if it is no longer possible to contemplate an operation of this kind, it is worth pausing for a moment to recall the magnitude of the effort which the Allies put forth on 6 June 1944. Allied aircraft flew 14,000 sorties during the night of 5 June and on D-Day. In these operations 127 aircraft were lost and 63 damaged.

More than 195,000 men were engaged in the ships and craft taking part in the naval operations. Over 23,000 airborne troops, about 8000 British and 15,000 American, were landed from the air. Total American casualties were 6000.

In the British sector the airborne troops and commandos had about 1300 casualties, including 100 glider pilots. Casualties among the seaborne troops were some 3000, of whom about 1000 were Canadians. Thus 156,215 troops were landed, from sea and air, in Normandy, and at a cost of some 10,300 casualties, broke Hitler's Atlantic Wall in a single day.

To one who had fought at Dunkirk and Dieppe it did seem that – at long last – our side had managed to get itself organized. In four years we had invented and mastered the intricate techniques of amphibious warfare. The road from the beaches of Normandy to the shores of the Baltic was a long one, and few indeed were to go the whole way. Still, they had got off to a good start.

RIGHT: *Sherman tanks negotiate the narrow streets of Normandy a few days after 6 June.*

APPENDIX

US D-Day Assault Divisions

Omaha Beach

1st US Division
116 Infantry
16 Infantry
18 Infantry
26 Infantry
115 Infantry
2nd Rangers
5th Rangers
741 Tank Battalion
111 Field Artillery Battalion
7 Field Artillery Battalion
81 Chemical Battalion

Utah Beach

4th US Division
8 Infantry
22 Infantry
12 Infantry
359 Infantry (attached from 90th Division)
70 Tank Battalion

British D-Day Assault Divisions

Sword Beach

3rd British Division
8th Brigade
1st Battalion The Suffolk Regiment
2nd Battalion The East Yorkshire Regiment
1st Battalion The South Lancashire Regiment
9th Brigade
2nd Battalion The Lincolnshire Regiment
1st Battalion The King's Own Scottish Borderers
2nd Battalion The Royal Ulster Rifles
185th Brigade
2nd Battalion The Royal Warwickshire Regiment
1st Battalion The Royal Norfolk Regiment
2nd Battalion The King's Shropshire Light Infantry
Divisional Troops
3rd Reconnaissance Regiment RAC
3rd Divisional Engineers
3rd Divisonal Signals
7th, 33rd and 76th Field, 20th Antitank and 92nd Light Antiaircraft Regiments RA
2nd Battalion The Middlesex Regiment (Machine Gun)

Juno Beach

3rd Canadian Division
7th Brigade
The Royal Winnipeg Rifles
The Regina Rifle Regiment
1st Battalion The Canadian Scottish Regiment
8th Brigade
The Queen's Own Rifles of Canada
Le Régiment de la Chaudière
The North Shore (New Brunswick) Regiment
9th Brigade
The Highland Light Infantry of Canada
The Stormont, Dundas and Glengarry Highlanders
The North Nova Scotia Highlanders
Divisional Troops
7th Reconnaissance Regiment (17th Duke of York's Royal Canadian Hussars)
3rd Canadian Divisional Engineers
3rd Canadian Divisional Signals
12th, 13th and 14th Field, 3rd Artillery and 4th Light Antiaircraft Regiments, RCA
The Cameron Highlanders of Ottawa (Machine Gun)

Gold Beach

50th British (Northumbrian) Division
69th Brigade
5th Battalion The East Yorkshire Regiment
6th and 7th Battalions The Green Howards
151st Brigade
6th, 8th and 9th Battalions The Durham Light Infantry
231st Brigade
2nd Battalion The Devonshire Regiment
1st Battalion The Hampshire Regiment
1st Battalion The Dorsetshire Regiment
Divisional Troops
61st Reconnaissance Regiment RAC
50th Divisional Engineers
50th Divisional Signals
74th, 90th and 124th Field, 102nd Antitank and 25th Light Anti-aircraft Regiments, RA
2nd Battalion The Cheshire Regiment (Machine Gun)

Other Formations

79th Armored Division
30th Armored Brigade
22nd Dragoons
1st Lothians and Border Horse
2nd County of London Yeomanry (Westminster Dragoons)
141st Regiment RAC
1st Tank Brigade
11th, 42nd and 49th Battalions RTR
1st Assault Brigade RE
5th, 6th and 42nd Assault Regiments RE
79th Armored Division Signals
1st Canadian Armored Personnel Carrier Regiment
1st Special Service Brigade
Nos 3, 4 and 6 Commandos
No 45 (Royal Marine) Commando
4th Special Service Brigade
Nos 41, 46, 47 and 48 (Royal Marine) Commandos
Royal Marine
Armored Support Group: 1st and 2nd Royal Marine Armored Support Regiments
Units of the Royal Artillery and Royal Engineers

Airborne Forces

6th Airborne Division
3rd Parachute Brigade
8th and 9th Battalions The Parachute Regiment
1st Canadian Parachute Battalion
5th Parachute Brigade
7th, 12th and 13th Battalions The Parachute Regiment
6th Airlanding Brigade
12th Battalion The Devonshire Regiment
2nd Battalion The Oxfordshire and Buckinghamshire Light Infantry
1st Battalion The Royal Ulster Rifles
Divisional Troops
6th Airborne Armored Reconnaissance Regiment RAC
6th Airborne Divisional Engineers
53rd Airlanding Light Regiment RA
6th Airborne Division Signals

US 101st Airborne Division
501st Parachute Infantry
502nd Parachute Infantry
506th Parachute Infantry
377th Parachute Field Artillery Battalion

US 82nd Airborne Division
505th Parachute Infantry
507th Parachute Infantry
508th Parachute Infantry

INDEX

Page numbers in *italics* refer to illustrations.

Air and sea bombardment 38-41, *39-41*, 44, 47, *62*
  maps *40, 50*
airborne operations 28-35, 38, 77
aircraft, Allied 14
  B-17 Flying Fortress *19*
  Dakota *32*
  Halifax 38
  Lancaster 38
  Lightning 39, *39*
  Marauder *39*, 40, *41*
  Mosquito 33, 38
  Mustang *18*
  Spitfire 39
  Stirling 33
  Thunderbolt 39
  Typhoon 60, *62*, 69
Ajax, HMS 40
Alexander, General Sir Harold *13*, 15
Allied (tactical) air forces 15, 18, 38, 39, 77
  2nd Tactical Air Force 69
Allied air superiority 8, 11, 39, 56, 72
Allied land forces
  12th Army Group 16
  21st Army Group
  dispositions of, map *54*
Allied supply lines *72-3, 75*
antitank weapons 28
Argonaut, HMS 40
Arkansas, USS *44*
Arnold, Commodore James 45
Arromanches les Bains 60, *76*
Atlantic Wall *11*, 24, 76, 77
Auchinleck, General Sir Claude 11

Baker, Maj Gen. Ray W 12
Battle of Britain 15
Bayerlein, Lt Gen. Fritz 68
Bayeux 21, 62, 75, 76
Belfast, HMS 61
Bénouville 28, 30, 32, 66, 67, 69
Bernières 62, 63, 64
Blumentritt, General Gunther 10
Bourne, General A G B 14
Bradley, Lt Gen. Omar N *15*, 16, *16*, 24, 72, *74*
British Army,
  First Canadian Army 16
  Second Army 16
  Fourth Army 19-20
    Corps
    XXX Corps *60*
    Royal Artillery 65
    Royal Engineers 65
    Divisions
    1st 64
    3rd Canadian 62, *63*, 78
    3rd Infantry 31, 32, 63, 64-5, 68, 69, 73, 78
    4th 64, 66
    6th Airborne *26-7*, 28, 32, 60, 66, 69, 76
    50th *60*, 61, 62, *62*, 78
    79th Armoured (the 'Funnies') 13 (caption), 78
    Brigades
    1st Special Service *21*, 28, 31, 32, *58-9*, 66, *66*, 69, 78
      see also under Commando units *and* Royal Marines
    3rd Parachute 28, *29*, 30-31, 78
    4th Special Service 60, 64, 65, *69*, 78
      see also under Royal Marines
    5th Parachute 29-30, 78
    7th Canadian 62, 78
    8th 65, 67, 68, 78
    8th Canadian 63, 78
    9th Canadian 63, 67, 68, 78
    9th 78
    30th Armoured 78
    56th 62
    69th 61, 78
    151st 61, 78

185th 67, 68, 78
231st 60, 78
    Regiments (British)
    1st Dorsetshire 61, 78
    4th/7th Dragoon Guards 61
    2nd East Yorkshire 65, 68, 78
    5th East Yorkshire 61
    6th Green Howards 61, 78
    7th Green Howards 61, 78
    1st Hampshire 60, 78
    1st Hussars 64
    13th/18th Hussars *25*, *64*, 65
    2nd King's Shropshire Light Infantry 67, 68, 69, 78
    9th Lancers 67
    Lincolnshire Regt 65, 78
    Nottinghamshire Yeomanry 61
    2nd Oxford and Bucks Light Infantry 28, 78
    9th Parachute Battalion 69, 78
    1st Royal Norfolk 67, 68, 78
    2nd Royal Warwickshire 68, 78
    1st South Lancashire 65, 78
    Staffordshire Yeomanry 67, 68
    1st Suffolk 68, 78
    Westminster Dragoons 61, 78
    others 78
    Regiments (Canadian)
    27th Canadian Armoured 63
    North Nova Scotia Highlanders 63, 78
    North Shore Regiment 62, 63, 78
    Queen's Own Rifles 62, 78
    Regina Rifles 62, 63, 78
    Winnipeg Rifles 62, 78
    others 78
    Commando units
    3 Commando 66, 73-4, 78
    4 Commando 78
    6 Commando 66, 78
    10 Inter-Allied Commando 65
    see also under Royal Marines
British Broadcasting Corporation 17
Brittany 20, 76
Brooke, General Sir Alan *13*
Bulolo, headquarters ship 40
Bures bridge 30, 32

Caen 20, 21, 22, 60, 67, 68, 69, 72, 73, 75, 76
Cairo Conference 12
Canham, Colonel (US Army) 56
Carentan 47, 74, 75, 76
Casablanca Conference 12, *13*
Cherbourg 20, 21, 72
Churchill, Winston S *13*, 14, *14, 28*
Churchill bridge-layer *66*
Colleville sur Mer 48, 51, 53, 56
Colleville sur Orne 67
Collins, Lt Gen. J L 44
Combined Operations headquarters 8, 14
Corry, USS, destroyer 44
COSSAC (Chief of Staff, Supreme Allied Command) 12-13, 14, 15
Cotenin peninsula 20, 21, *32*, 32-3, 34, 38, 44, 72, 74
Crerar, Lt Gen. Henry D G 16
Cross-Channel Attack (Harrison) 33
Cunningham, Admiral Sir Andrew *13*

D-Day (Tute) 33
de Gaulle, General Charles 17
deception plans (Allied) 18-20, 38
Dempsey, Lt Gen. Sir Miles 16, 24, 68, 72
Diadem, HMS 63
Dieppe raid, 1942 8, *9-10*, 11, 66, 76
Dives river 28, 32, 33
Dollmann, General Friedrich 68, 74
DUKW amphibious truck *46*, 50
Dunkirk evacuation 15, 64

Eden, Anthony 13
Eisenhower, General Dwight D 12, *13*, 14, 15, *15*, 16, *18*, 24, 25, *28-9*
El Alamein, Battle of 11
Ellis, L F 31
Emerald, HMS 60

Falley, General 35
Feuchtinger, Lt Gen. Edgar 22, 68, 72-3, 75
France, 1940 campaign in 9, 10, 11

Gale, Maj Gen. Richard N 30
Gamelin, General Maurice 11
George VI, King 24
German Army,
  strength and disposition of 11-12, 20, 22, 72, 75-6
    map *54*
  Army Group B 11, 23, 68, 73
  Seventh Army 68, 69, 73, 74
  I SS Panzer Corps 68
  LXXXIV Corps 22, 34, 38, 73, 75
    Divisions
    6th Parachute 47
    7th Panzer 10
    12th SS Panzer 22, 68
    21st Panzer 20, 22, 30, 63, 68, 69, 72, 73, 75, 76
    77th Field 22, 76
    84th Field 76
    91st Air Landing 20, 33, 35
    91st Infantry 46
    116th Panzer 22
    352nd Infantry 22, 47, 57, 75
    353rd 76
    709th Infantry 22, 47
    711th 22
    716th Infantry 22, 28, 34, 62, 69, 75
    Panzer *Lehr* 20, 22, 68
    Regiments
    6th Parachute 20, 74, 75
    125th Panzer Grenadier 30
    171st Artillery 63
    726th Infantry 63
    736th Grenadier 28, 30, 63, 64, 67
    915th Infantry 62, 75
German defense preparations 8, 10, *10*, 11-12, *12-13*, 20-22, 75-6
German Navy 39
  Naval Group West 12
German OKW 35
Gerow, Lt Gen. L T 44
gliders 28, *29*, 30, 31, *31*, 32, *32-3*, 46, 69, 75
Gold beach 60, *60*

Hall, Rear Admiral J L 44, 51, *74*
Harrison, G A 33
Heydte, Major F-E Freiherr von der 74-5
Hitler, Adolf 8-11 *passim*, 19, 20, 24
Hobart, Maj Gen. Sir Percy 76
Hollis, Sgt Maj. S E 61
Howard, Major R J 28, 30
Huebner, Maj Gen. C R 56

Italian campaign 8, 14, 15, 16, 66

Jodl, General Alfred 20
Juno beach 63, 64

Keitel, Field Marshal Wilhelm 35, 72
Keyes, Admiral of the Fleet Sir Roger 14
Kieffer, Commandant 65
Kirk, Rear Admiral A 24-5, 44, *74*
Kraiss, General Dietrich 75
Krancke, Vice-Admiral 12, 23, 39

La Brêche 65, 66, 67
landing craft 14, *23*, *25*, 40, *42-3*, 44, *45*, 47, 49, *49*, 50-51, *52*, 60, 62
  Landing Craft, Assault (LCA) *6-7*
  Landing Craft, Infantry (LCI) *38*, *52*, 66, *74*
  Landing Craft, Tank (LST) 67
Langrune sur Mer 60, 64
Laurent sur Mer 48, 53, 56
Laval, Pierre 17
Le Hamel 60, 61-2
Le Port village 30
Leigh-Mallory, Air Chief Marshal Sir Trafford 15, *15*, 25
Lion sur Mer 60, 65
Longues battery 38, 40
Lovat, Brigadier Lord 32, 69

Luftwaffe 12, 15

MacArthur, General Douglas 14
Marcks, General Erich 22, 34, 57, 73, 75
Marshall, General George C *13*, 14
Martin, Major J E 67
Meise, Doctor Wilhelm *12*
Merville battery 28, 29, 31-2, 38
Montgomery, General Sir Bernard 11, *13*, 14, 15, *15-16*, 16, *18*, 24, 25, 64, 72
Morgan, Lt Gen. Frederick E 12-13, 14
Mountbatten, Vice-Admiral Lord Louis 8, 14
Mulberry harbor 76, *76*

Nevada, USS *36-7, 41*, 51
North African campaigns 11, 14, 15, 16, 66
Norway, fictitious invasion plans 18, 19

Omaha beach 34, 44, 46, 47-53, *49, 52-5*, 56-7, *57, 70-71*, 75, 76
Oppeln-Bronowski, Colonel von 75
Orion, HMS 61
Orne river 28, 29, 32, 33, 34, 60, 68
Otway, Lt Col. Terence 31-2
Ouistreham 32, 38, *58-9*, 60, 65, 66, 68

Paratroopers *26-31, 33-5*, 44, 75
Pas de Calais 18, 20, 24, 35, 75
Patton, Lt Gen. George S 14, 15, 16, *16*
Pemsel, Maj Gen. Max 72
Pétain, Marshal Henri 17
PLUTO (Pipe Line Under The Ocean) 76
Pointe du Hoe *56*, 57
Port en Bessin 44, 60, *69, 75*
preparations (Allied) *2-3, 6-7*, 12-16, 17-18, *18-24*
 map *23*
Pyle, Ernie 16

Quadrant Conference, Quebec 14, *14*
Queen beach 60, 65

Ramillies, HMS 39, 40, 66
Ramsay, Admiral Sir Bertram 15, *15*, 25
Ranville 28, 30, 69

Rennie, Maj Gen. T G 65
Resistance forces 17, 34, 74
Richter, Lt Gen. W 34
Ridgway, General Matthew B 33, 35
Roberts, HMS 39
Rommel, Field Marshal Erwin 8, 10-11, *12*, 16, 24, 60, 69, 72, 75
Roosevelt, President Franklin D 12, 14, *14*
Roosevelt, Brigadier General Theodore 45
Roseveare, Major J C A 30
Royal Air Force 15, 68
 Air Defense of Great Britain 33
 Bomber Command 33, 38
Royal Marines 14
 41 Commando 60, 65, 78
 45 Commando 32, 66, 78
 46 Commando 60, 78
 47 Commando 60, 78
 48 Commando 60, 64, 78
 Armoured Support Regiment 66, 78
Royal Naval Volunteer Reserve 66
Royal Navy 53
Rundstedt, Field Marshal Karl Gerd von *8*, 8-10, 11, 16, 20, 21, 24, 35, 72, 75, 76

St Croix sur Mer 62, 63
St Lô 21-2, 34
St Nazaire, raid on, 1942 8
Ste Mère Eglise 34, *34*, 45, 46, 74
Satterlee, USS 57
Sicily campaign 8, 14, 15, 16, 28, 66
Smith, Lt Gen. W Bedell 15, *15*
Special Operations Executive (SOE) 17
Speidel, General Hans 72
Sperrle, Field Marshal Hugo 12
Svenner, Norwegian warship 40
Sword beach *58-9*

Talybont, HMS 57
tanks 64, *76-7*
 amphibious (DD) 44, 49, *54*, 61, 62, 65, *65, 77*
 'flail' tanks 61
 'Funnies' 61, 76
Tedder, Air Chief Marshal Sir Arthur *13*, 14-15, *15*, 25

Texas, USS *36-7*
Thorne, Lt Gen. Sir A F A N 19
Time Magazine 33
Trident Conference, Washington 13
Tute, Warren 33

United States Air Force,
 Eighth Air Force *19*
 Ninth Air Force 40, *41*
United States Army,
 First Army 16, 33
 Third Army 16
 V Corps 44, 46, 57
 VII Corps 44, 46
  Divisions
 1st Infantry *2-3, 45, 51*, 53, 56, 78
 3rd Armored *18*
 4th Infantry 44, 45, *48*, 78
 8th Infantry 75
 29th 53, 56
 82nd Airborne 29 (caption), 32, 33-4, *34*, 45, 46, 78
 101st Airborne 28, 32, *32*, 33, 34, 46, 47, 75, 78
  Regiments
 116th Infantry 51, 78
 Rangers *10, 20, 50*, 56, *56*
 others 78
United States Coast Guard *38*
United States Navy 53
 IX Troop Carrier Command 33
 Western Task Force 44
Utah beach 34, 40, 44-6, *46*, 47, 48, 74-5

Vehicles, amphibious (Duplex Drive) *47, 49*
Victory in the West (Ellis) 31
Vierville sur Mer 48, 53, 56

Warspite, HMS 39, 40
Whitworth, Lieutenant P 66

ACKNOWLEDGMENTS

The author and publishers would like to thank Martin Bristow for designing this book and Moira Dykes for the picture research. The following agencies and individuals provided photographic material:

Bison Picture Library: pages 8, 11(both), 15, 19(top), 42-43, 46(below), 50, 51(top right), 57(both), 62(top), 63(below), 64(top), 69(below).
Bundesarchiv: pages 12(top), 33(top)
John Frost Newspapers: page 67 (below).
Hulton-Deutsch Collection: page 74(below).
Imperial War Museum: pages 9(both), 10, 12(below), 13(both), 16(both), 17(both), 20(below), 21(both), 25(top), 26-27, 29(below), 40(top), 47(top), 58-59, 65(below), 66(below), 76(top), 77(both).
Peter Newark's Military Pictures: page 55.

Robert Hunt Picture Library: pages 5, 20(top), 24(both), 30(right), 31(below), 32(below), 35(below), 40(below), 41(below), 45(top), 46(top), 47(below), 60, 61(below), 63(top), 64(below), 76(below).
The Research House: pages 2-3, 22(top right)/**Dakota:** 30(left)/**Department of Defense:** 22(top left), 25(below), 33(below), 48(both), 51(top left)/**Imperial War Museum:** 61(top), 62(below), 65(top), 66(top), 68, 69(top), 75(both)/**US Army:** 31(top), 34(both), 35(top), 53(below), 72/**US National Archives:** 23/**US Navy:** 6-7, 22(below), 51(below), 54, 74(top).
US Air Force: pages 18(below), 32(top), 39(both).
US Army: pages 18(top), 19(below), 28, 29(top), 56(top).
US Coast Guard: pages 38(below), 45(below), 49(top), 67(top).
US National Archives: pages 53(top), 56(below).
US Navy: pages 14, 36-37, 41(top), 44, 49(below), 52(both), 70-71, 73(both).